The Chieftain and the Chair

The

THE RISE OF

Chieftain

DANISH DESIGN IN

and the

POSTWAR AMERICA

Chair

Maggie Taft

The University of Chicago Press
Chicago and London

The University of Chicago Press, Chicago 60637
The University of Chicago Press, Ltd., London
Published 2023
Printed in China

32 31 30 29 28 27 26 25 24 23   1 2 3 4 5

ISBN-13: 978-0-226-55032-9 (cloth)
ISBN-13: 978-0-226-55046-6 (e-book)
DOI: https://doi.org/10.7208/chicago/9780226550466.001.0001

The Neil Harris Endowment Fund was established in 2008 to support the publication of heavily illustrated, historically significant books. The Fund honors the
innovative scholarship of Neil Harris, the Preston and Sterling Morton Professor
Emeritus of History and Art History at the University of Chicago, and it is supported
by contributions from the students, colleagues, and friends of Neil Harris.

Library of Congress Cataloging-in-Publication Data

Names: Taft, Maggie, author.
Title: The chieftain and the chair : the rise of Danish design in postwar America /
    Maggie Taft.
Description: Chicago : The University of Chicago Press, 2023. | Includes bibliograph-
    ical references and index.
Identifiers: LCCN 2022049679 | ISBN 9780226550329 (cloth) | ISBN 9780226550466
    (ebook)
Subjects: LCSH: Furniture design—Denmark—History—20th century. | Furniture
    design—United States—History—20th century.
Classification: LCC NK2585 .T34 2023 | DDC 749.09489—dc23/eng/20221109
LC record available at https://lccn.loc.gov/2022049679

♾ This paper meets the requirements of ANSI/NISO Z39.48-1992
(Permanence of Paper).

In furniture, handmade or manufactured, the Danes stand like a Colossus over all of Europe and indeed reach a long arm into our own country.

DAVID AND MARIAN GREENBERG,
The Shopping Guide to Europe (1954)

Contents

Figure 0.1 Edith Farnsworth House dining area with Hans Wegner's Round Chairs, 1955. Courtesy the Edith Farnsworth House, a site of the National Trust for Historic Preservation. Photographer unknown.

Introduction

1955. Plano, Illinois. Alongside the Fox River, in a tree-lined clearing, a glass house hovers on stilts. Inside, a pair of Hans Wegner's Round Chairs dresses the ends of a dining table set for six (fig. 0.1). The chairs' gentle contours stand in contrast to the right angles of the building's planes, yet their silhouettes echo the transparency of the floating glass walls. Light streams through their open teakwood frames and cane seats. An ocean away from Denmark, where they were designed and made, the chairs seem at home.

When Dr. Edith Farnsworth chose Wegner's Round Chair—often called simply "the Chair"—for this prominent place in the country retreat Ludwig Mies van der Rohe had designed for her, refusing the tubular steel and leather pieces of his own design that he proposed, she was but one of many Americans embracing the midcentury fad for Scandinavian design. Danish design, in particular, became so popular that American manufacturers sought to capitalize on its cachet. As Danish furniture exports to the United States climbed over the course of the 1950s, American furniture companies hired Danes to design lines of modern furnishings. Some companies even referenced the craze in their names. Dansk, for example, was not a Danish company but an American one, which sometimes hired Danes to design its dinner- and cookware. Lifestyle editors featured Danish design in full-color magazine spreads, and "Danish" became shorthand for a livable, modern style associated with natural materials, quality craftsmanship, and casual comfort. According to George Tanier, who began importing Danish design immediately after World War II, "It addressed the needs of younger couples and new households, with its cleanliness of design."[1] Looking back on the period in the 1990s, a reporter for the *New York Times* would refer to it as *the design movement of the 1950s.*[2]

Though "Danish design" appears to describe a national style, it is not interchangeable with midcentury design from Denmark. Period participants in the furniture industry understood this, even as they benefited from the publicity and growth in sales that the term and its associated aesthetic produced. "We cannot say that a Danish taste of furnishing is existing," one prominent furniture maker told an Italian journalist in 1955, as Danish furniture exports skyrocketed.[3] Americans and other foreigners, he argued, were conflating all of Denmark's production with one small, Copenhagen-based sliver of the industry; furniture like Wegner's Chair, though seen as representative of Danish design at large, existed alongside industrial design and folk art, neohistoricist homage and Viking-inspired kitsch. But the Italian journalist was skeptical of the furniture maker's protest. "Danish taste must exist," he wrote, "for the simple reason that millions of persons are convinced of its existence."

The Danish furniture maker was correct to insist that Denmark had no single, unified design identity; its overseas exports represented neither the full range of Danish design production nor a design style embraced by all of Denmark's nearly 4.5 million midcentury inhabitants. Nonetheless, as the Italian reporter countered, widespread belief in the idea of Danish design was enough to make it real. The version of Danish design embraced by Americans, in the postwar era and today, may have been a fiction, but its emergence as something recognizable and powerful shaped design culture and popular taste worldwide. How did this happen, and why?

The Chieftain and the Chair answers these questions by following two iconic designs—Finn Juhl's Chieftain Chair and Hans Wegner's Round Chair—from their conception and fabrication in Denmark to their popularization and reproduction in the United States (plates 1 and 2). The Chieftain was, as described in the *New York Times*, one of the "status chairs" of the 1950s.[4] And the Chair was a media darling, appearing in a variety of contexts, including magazine features on interior design and the first televised presidential debate. The Chieftain and the Chair are both notable design achievements, as well. Though the Chieftain's size makes it something of an outlier in a category typified by small, limber designs, its biomorphic form is emblematic of what *House Beautiful* called the "soft, rounded flowing forms" of Danish design.[5] With its wooden frame suspending its upholstered seat back and armrests, it also exemplifies a structural technique often deployed by Juhl to produce a floating effect. The joinery of Wegner's Chair is innovative, with its unbroken top rail transitioning into armrests and elegant finger joints providing structural strength that eliminates the need for a supporting backboard.

Even so, the two chairs are less exceptional than exemplary products of Danish design in the postwar period. Their stories help to show how Danish design's popularization was the product not simply of creative genius, but of institutions, designers, fabricators, distributors, professional and amateur tastemakers, and, perhaps most surprisingly, copyists, who together brought the very idea of Danish design into existence. This diffuse activity is not unique to Danish design; understanding design history requires attending to the contexts that give shape to objects, the conditions of their manufacture, the circumstances of their circulation, and how they are taken up by the market and by consumers. Here, the Chieftain and the Chair, two familiar designs, tell the particular story of Danish Modern's invention and rise in postwar America.

One peculiar aspect of the midcentury Danish design craze in the United States is the extent to which the idea dwarfs the reality. Between 1950 and 1955, Danish furniture exports to the United States increased more than thirtyfold, yet the total numbers were modest.[6] European imports accounted for only one-half of 1 percent of America's more than four-billion-dollar furniture industry, and furniture from Denmark represented only 10 percent of that (about two million dollars), a market share much smaller than that of, for example, design from Italy.[7] And most of the furniture Denmark exported to the United States was expensive. Not everyone who bought it could, like Edith Farnsworth, afford to commission a preeminent architect to design a country house, but they did tend to be wealthy enough to spend at least $125 on a Wegner Chair. (At that price, a set of eight would have cost a third as much as a Ford Thunderbird, the bestselling car in America in 1955.) So even as exports grew, the actual number of Danish chairs, tables, and other furniture pieces traveling across the ocean and arriving in US homes remained rather small. American-made furniture designed in a so-called Danish or Danish Modern style was far more prevalent.

Nevertheless, the American "discovery" of Danish design, as Danish furniture maker A. J. Iversen called it, was transformative.[8] It helped popularize Danish design around the globe and grew the export market far beyond what anyone in the industry had imagined possible. To call it a discovery by America, however, is a misnomer. As this book shows, the Danish furniture industry deliberately targeted the American market. Danish organizations and individuals strategically developed and deployed marketing narratives to sell the furniture in the United States.[9] And Danish designers and furniture makers conceived and adjusted their designs with the American market in mind. This was not an unprecedented strategy; Chinese pottery manufacturers, for example, after trade routes were established by the Portuguese and the Dutch in the sixteenth century, made porcelain specifically for European and, later, American markets. In the case of postwar Denmark, furniture for export reshaped multiple aspects of the domestic industry, from design details to production models. In other words, Danish design was not merely embraced by Americans. It was *made for Americans*.

After World War II, Danish furniture professionals sought to grow their industry by prioritizing exports and targeting the American market. Furniture exports supported the goal of diversifying the national economy. Immediately after the war, Denmark's economy depended on Britain, the largest importer of Danish pork and dairy. But volatile markets made this risky. When Britain devalued its currency in 1949, for example, Denmark felt the reverberations and was forced to do the same. Furniture production had been largely uninterrupted by the war, and the industry was well positioned to participate in economic diversification.

Initially, Danish manufacturers targeted Europe. With knockdown designs that shipped flat to be assembled at home, Denmark, they imagined, could furnish the houses and apartments being rebuilt across the continent. But by the end of the 1940s, it was clear that the American market was far more robust. Returning soldiers were buying houses with government support and needed furniture to fill them. While Europe was rebuilding with American dollars, the US was building anew with a flush economy. Suburbs grew at a staggering rate in the decade and a half after World War II. In 1945, 325,000 new homes were built. The following year that number more than tripled, and it continued to rise each year until 1950, when it reached nearly two million before leveling off.[10] In the decade or so after World War II, spending on home furnishings and appliances shot up by 240 percent.[11] In short, Americans wanted new furniture and had the money to buy it. Danish designers, makers, and retailers made the most of the opportunity, often working with others in the region to amplify their force.

With support from the Danish government, professional organizations like the Danish Society of Arts and Crafts and Industrial Design partnered with those in Sweden, Norway, and Finland to grow exports through coordinated strategies. Postwar collaborations included *Design in Scandinavia*, a landmark exhibition that traveled to twenty-three institutions across North America between 1953 and 1957, and the Scandinavian Design Cavalcade, which drew foreign tourists to the region for an annual autumn lineup of design events. These cultural collaborations built upon prewar regional exchanges but stemmed primarily from economic exigency. For example, the participating countries were responsible for all costs associated with planning *Design in Scandinavia* and shipping the exhibited objects to the United States. In 1953, no one Nordic country could have funded such an enterprise.

Collaboration allowed the Nordic countries to pool their resources in a variety of ways. It was not only a matter of sharing expenses or offering tourists a larger menu of design events from which to sample. Production operated at such a smaller scale in the Nordic countries than it did in America that serving the US market presented a challenge. For example, the Norwegian company Norway Designs for Living, which exported goods to a roaming pop-up shop with stops in Chicago, Minneapolis, Seattle, and Grand Forks, North Dakota, lasted only briefly because Norway's production capacity could not meet the US demand.[12] Collaboration helped the Nordic countries more easily supply the American market, and stores like Georg Jensen in New York, Design Research in Cambridge, Massachusetts, Contemporary Backgrounds in Detroit, Baldwin Kingrey in Chicago, Zacho in Los Angeles, and Cargoes in San Francisco showcased design from across the region, even if, as in the case of Georg Jensen of Denmark, the shop was specifically affiliated with one nation.

Through their various collaborations, the Nordic countries presented America with the idea of Scandinavian design as "a cultural and regional unit," in the words of the *Design in Scandinavia* exhibition catalog, with an aesthetic described by Museum of Modern Art curator Edgar Kaufmann Jr. as "clean, well-finished, unobtrusive, carefully considered, ingenious, sensible and elegant."[13] Yet Denmark's specific story is distinctive. Though "Danish design" may have been invented to serve the American market, Danish institutions, policies, and laws gave shape to that invention, molding it in ways that distinguished it from Scandinavian design writ large. Teak, for example, was commonly used in the furniture that came to be known as Danish as well as in other Scandinavian design. But it had a unique importance in Denmark, which did not have enough native wood to serve the growing export market; teak, however, was readily accessible because of Denmark's colonial relationship with Thailand. The situation was very different in the other Nordic countries, where native woods were widely available. Though the rise of Scandinavian design contributed to the popularization of Danish design, the two categories are not interchangeable. Denmark's story, like those of each of the other Nordic countries, is specific.[14]

The Chieftain and the Chair focuses on Denmark because Danish design, more than Swedish, Norwegian, or Finnish design, emerged with a distinctive force in the postwar period, especially in the United States. Danish furniture, in particular, captured the American imagination. American companies like Heywood-Wakefield and Magnavox made furniture they called "Danish," *not* Scandinavian.

In the 1950s, Finn Juhl and Hans Wegner were two of Danish design's biggest names on both sides of the Atlantic, and the Chieftain and the Chair were, respectively, their most recognizable designs. As the creators of two of the first pieces of furniture exported to the United States as Danish design, they served as emissaries. Yet their paths were not entirely parallel. Juhl and Wegner were part of the same Copenhagen-based design scene, but their different backgrounds and training offer insight into the disparate institutions that structured the furniture scene and the historical context that shaped it. The Chieftain and the Chair were, moreover, made to circulate overseas in very different ways, demonstrating how the postwar popularity of Danish design owed not only to "good design" and a master marketing campaign but also to intentional and divergent strategies for establishing commercial partnerships and designing for the American market.

Once in the United States, the Chieftain and the Chair took on lives of their own, recast by tastemakers and consumers who latched on to different aspects of the designs and produced new narratives around them. For example, while Danish sellers pitched the furniture as part of a handmade tradition distinct from modern industrial production, American curators and editors variously heralded it as mirroring American practice or providing a model for it. The Chieftain, which had made a splash in the Danish furniture scene, left little impression on the American market, while the Chair took it by storm. These new narratives remade the definition of Danish design, a definition then codified by manufacturers seeking to capitalize on the trend. Piracy helped bolster the mainstream popularity of Danish design as a style, while at the same time radically

INTRODUCTION

transforming the furniture industry in Denmark and ultimately undermining its export market. The stories of the Chieftain and the Chair offer a window into the broader history of Danish design and show that, far from a homegrown creation, Danish design was made through exchange.

: : :

"Who can force Americans to love Danish furniture?" Finn Juhl would ask a *New York Times* reporter in 1977, after the Danish design fad had faded.[15] Looking around a New York City furniture store filled with "Egyptian baroque" (Juhl's description) and "packing-crate modern" (the reporter's), he posed the question rhetorically, and with a hint of regret.[16] Taste was taste, his question implied, and nobody could be made to like what they didn't. But the story of popular taste is neither as simple nor as inexplicable as Juhl's question would suggest. While midcentury Americans were not forced to buy Danish furniture, a host of factors encouraged them to do so.

In stores and museum exhibitions and on the pages of magazines, Danish design specifically, and Scandinavian design more generally, was presented as a coherent and totalizing aesthetic. But in the world beyond, it coexisted with other kinds of design, modern and otherwise. Edith Farnsworth, for example, placed her Round Chairs in an International Style house, a combination that would have been unimaginable in the pages of *House Beautiful*, which lauded Scandinavian design as "human and warm" while deriding the International Style as "totalitarian."[17] Though neither the Chieftain nor the Chair was mass-produced, many of each were sold to people across the United States. Some placed them in high-rise apartments, some in suburban ranches. Some paired them with other modern furnishings, others with pieces inherited from generations past. The recorded histories of the Chieftain and the Chair provide insight into how and why Danish design came to figure so prominently in postwar American culture, but they tell only part of the story. The other part is kept in private living rooms, captured in family photographs, and archived in personal memories. *The Chieftain and the Chair* aims to enrich those dispersed histories by giving them context. But it is because those personal accounts are so many and so beloved by those who carry them that the book was written in the first place.

Copenhagen's Design Community

To hear Finn Juhl tell it, the idea for the Chieftain came to him in a flash.

Late one morning in the spring of 1949, he was struck by the desire for a comfortable reading chair. He sketched four vertical lines on a scrap of paper no larger than a postage stamp. By the time he went to bed, he had mocked up the plans, rendering the burly design in delicate watercolor.[1]

This creation myth—the design emerging from his mind fully formed, a direct expression of his personal experience—fits neatly into Juhl's cultivated reputation as an artist. He liked to say that his furniture was like sculpture, drawing its sinuous form from ancient Cycladic figures as well as the modern work of contemporaries like British sculptors Barbara Hepworth and Henry Moore.[2] To make the comparison explicit, in exhibitions he would often pair his work with sculptures by Jean Arp and Erik Thommesen and paintings by Vilhelm Lundstrøm and Asger Jorn. The local press advanced the analogy by, for example, lauding his "simplicity of line like that a painter might use to describe a nude."[3] It was—and continues to be—said that in his youth Juhl told his disapproving father that he wished to be an art historian, further cementing the idea that his creativity was informed by and aligned with the annals of art.[4]

In the case of the Chieftain, with its back suspended between two stiles and its seat and armrests appearing to float, he emphatically insisted upon the work's status as art. When Juhl debuted the design at an exhibition in the fall of 1949, he presented the chair alongside a careful selection of artifacts that included a seashell, a butterfly, an archer's bow, a photograph of an African hunter wielding a spear, and a thick slice of a tree trunk hung vertically on the wall, like a picture (fig. 1.1). The display knowingly employed modern art's familiar references to the natural and the native, as if to write Juhl's design into a lineage that included Matisse, Picasso, and others who claimed the so-called primitive as a source of inspiration.

His chair's name reiterates the point. As the story goes, a journalist proposed calling the thronelike seat the "King's Chair" after the Danish king, Frederick IX, sat in it at the exhibition's opening, but Juhl suggested Chieftain's Chair instead, eschewing the pomp of royalty in favor of a romantic—and colonizing—view of primitive authenticity. Unfortunately, there are no images of the king in the chair to support this narrative, and, in fact, the chair's name was not so immediately fixed; in 1959, a decade after its debut, a Copenhagen department store advertised it as Arm Chair.[5] But the name "the Chieftain" taps into a modernist trope that was, by 1949, well established across Europe and mobilized by Danish artists including Jorn, Carl-Henning Pedersen, and the other members of the avant-garde collective Helhesten (the Hell-Horse), with whom Juhl had collaborated on an experimental 1944 exhibition. Eager to assert the chair's relation to modern painting and sculpture, he could sometimes during the 1949 exhibition's run be found seated in the Chief-

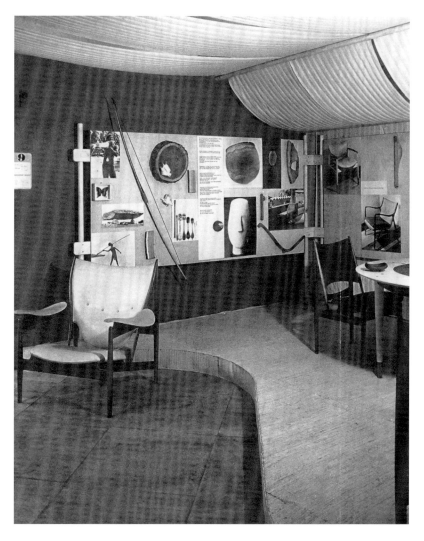

Figure 1.1 Niels Vodder display featuring furniture designed by Finn Juhl, Cabinetmakers Guild Exhibition, 1949. Photograph: Aage Strüwing, © Jørgen Strüwing.

tain, talking with visitors about abstract art and furniture design.[6] His watercolor plans for the display insist upon the connection, specifying that the Chieftain and a sofa version (often referred to as the double Chieftain) be exhibited "in a context that can explain and emphasize their form and consistency with other artistic phenomena and with the natural occurrences that foster the imagination and the indelible teachings and pleasures of shapes, lines, colors, materials" (plate 3). The Chieftain, these display notes declare, did not merely resemble art. It *was* art.

And yet, when Juhl was asked about the Chieftain's origins in the early 1980s, more than three decades after its conception, he confessed that the chair arose from something other than a simple stroke of genius. "It may have been that I had it in mind as a vague idea that I would like to make a big chair," he allowed. "There were so many small handy chairs."[7] This offhand remark suggests that the Chieftain was not only designed to be in conversation with modern art. It was also a deliberate intervention into a broader design culture. The Chieftain was a response.

Beyond amending a frequently repeated story, Juhl's admission suggests that the design owed as much to his participation in a creative community as it did to his singular creativity. That community, with its predilection for small, handy chairs, was defined not only by individuals but by institutions. A pair of Copenhagen schools, one training architects and the other cabinetmakers, centered Denmark's modern furniture community in the nation's capital and established its underlying tenets. Indeed, the exhibition where Juhl debuted the Chieftain was an annual event, bringing together graduates from these schools to imagine new furniture pieces and styles. Together, this community helped invent the very idea of Danish design.

A City Transformed

In the autumn of 1949, when the Chieftain premiered, Finn Juhl was working two jobs. At his drawing office in Nyhavn, Copenhagen's postcard-ready canal lined with brightly colored buildings, he and his small staff turned out plans for furniture, exhibitions, and store displays. At Skolen for Boligindretning (School of Interior Design) in Frederiksberg, a tony municipality nestled within Copenhagen's west side, he was beginning his fourth year as dean. Though thirty-seven, his soft and youthful face framed by a pronounced widow's peak and sharp chin made him look not much older than his students. While most were well-to-do young women who would use what they learned to design their own tasteful homes, Juhl plucked a few to work in his office. (He hired Marianne Riis-Carstensen, for example, to make his watercolors, though it was always Juhl's name that was signed to them.) Other students went on to make names for themselves in the field of design: Arne Vodder would specialize in furniture for export; Henry Klein, a Norwegian, would develop a pioneering method for molding plastic, later used in Denmark to manufacture Arne Jacobsen's Egg Chair; and Bodil Kjær would establish herself as a designer of office furnishings, including a desk—she called it a "working table"—made famous, in part, by its appearance in three James Bond films.

Both of the neighborhoods in which Juhl worked had been formative for him. He had been raised in Frederiksberg, and studied architecture at the prestigious Kongelige Danske Kunstakademi, Arkitektskole (Royal Danish Academy of Fine Arts, School of Architecture), housed in Charlottenborg Palace, just down the street from his office. But if the neighborhoods were familiar from his youth, they were hardly unchanged. In the years since he finished school in 1934, economic depression, urban development, and war had transformed the city.

In 1949, when Juhl designed the Chieftain, the urban fabric was pregnant with the legacy of Nazi occupation. Walking along Nyhavn canal to its terminus at Kongens Nytorv, the city's largest public square, one could be forgiven for seeing the equestrian statue at the square's center and thinking not of the seventeenth-century Danish king on whom it was modeled but of Denmark's wartime king, Christian X. After Germany invaded, he circled the square each day atop his horse. Promenading through the streets unchaperoned, for citizens and occupiers alike to see, his rides demonstrated official resistance amid the forced acquiescence of Nazi rule. This open display of defiance hints at Denmark's unusual war story. Though Germany invaded in the spring of 1940, exploiting Denmark's ports and agricultural resources to buttress Nazi military might, it was another three years before the invaders placed their northern neighbor under direct military occupation. In the interim, Denmark maintained sovereign control over domestic politics, police, and courts and protected its Jewish population, first refusing to pass anti-Jewish laws and then, in the autumn of 1943, ferrying Jews to safety in neutral Sweden after German authorities ordered their arrest and internment. Denmark was not a silent collaborator.

Resistance in the form of direct political and military action as well as symbolic displays of defiance was pervasive, though legends have been folded into the historical record. According to lore, King Christian X not only took his daily rides but also wore an armband with the Star of David, the symbol the Nazis used to mark the Jews. While there is no evidence of this, Den Permanente, a Copenhagen design store that would later carry the Chieftain, did wear the star, in a manner of speaking: the shop illustrated its Christmas 1942 newspaper advertisement with two large, text-filled Stars of David. "Under the stars' gentle and ancient symbol," read the ad's copy, "we have gathered items to create a festive Christmas." By using the symbol of the star, the furniture store expressed solidarity with the persecuted.[8]

That Den Permanente was advertising a holiday collection in the first place—that there were furniture pieces, ceramics, glass, silver, and textiles to fill its shelves—offers insight into life in Denmark during the war. While Jews, including architect Arne Jacobsen and Kaj Dessau, founder of the important interwar furniture store BO, were forced into exile, most Danes carried on with daily life. Designers kept designing. Fabricators continued producing. Schools remained open, except for a few months in the autumn of 1943, when students were encouraged to help in the effort to ferry the country's Jews across Øresund's brackish waters to Sweden. That year, the Danish furniture company Fritz Hansen was less concerned with bombs than with a catastrophic cold spell that had damaged many of the country's native walnut trees.[9] Apart from the island of Bornholm, bombed by the Soviets in 1945, Denmark emerged from the war with its landscape and its industry largely unscathed.

Juhl's own wartime experience was characterized by professional success. He was employed in architect Vilhelm Lauritzen's design studio, then at work on two large projects that have since emerged as its most renowned: the first Copenhagen airport and Radiohuset, the Danish Broadcasting Corporation's headquarters, for which Juhl designed many of the furnishings and interior fixtures. He was also establishing his own name, regularly designing and exhibiting new furniture that was lauded by critics in Denmark's daily newspapers. And in 1942, when many in

Europe were exiled, imprisoned, or displaced, he designed his own first house, a spacious, L-shaped bungalow.

Juhl built the house for himself and his wife, Inge-Marie Skaarup (they later divorced), on a plot of land in Ordrup, a leafy town five miles north of Copenhagen. Into the early twentieth century, it had been a farming village and popular destination for weekend travelers seeking a pastoral retreat from city life. During Juhl's youth in the teens and twenties, it was developed, the farmland divided and built up with apartment buildings and single-family houses. In 1924, a train station opened, serving the area's newcomers and beckoning the arrival of more, Juhl among them.

Ordrup's conversion from farm town to suburb is emblematic of a broader transformation that occurred in Denmark's rural communities between the wars. While Ordrup was reconfigured by suburban sprawl, many others were hollowed out by economic collapse. In 1919 a land reform measure partitioned parish land, which made up most of the country, and distributed the parcels among independent farming families, giving them rights over their labor and their harvest but also requiring them to take on the financial risk of operating independently. When aftershocks of the 1929 stock market crash in the United States hit Europe, that risk became devastating. Agricultural prices fell in Britain and Germany, the two largest importers of Danish foodstuffs, and Danish farmers raced to increase production to make up for lost profits. But flooding the market only led to further fallout. Farmers went bankrupt, sold their farms, and fled the countryside, seeking jobs in the city. The effect of this migration inverted national demographics: in 1930, roughly half of the Danish workforce labored in agriculture and 30 percent in industry; ten years later, those numbers were reversed.[10] But the nation's economy did not evolve to mirror the demographic shift. Dairy and pork remained its most lucrative exports. At the end of the war, Denmark retained its reputation overseas as, in the words of one American journalist, the "Delicatessen of Europe," a description that, if charming on its face, bore a sinister resonance—the Nazis had relied on the deli that was Denmark to keep their soldiers fed.[11]

Though the agricultural foundation of the Danish economy remained, life was nonetheless changed, particularly in the capital, where the newcomers arriving daily sought not only jobs but places to live. Housing became a central concern for politicians and architects alike, and was a core subject of study during Juhl's time at the Royal Academy, where he trained under the architect Kay Fisker. Juhl began there in 1930, eight years after Fisker completed the Hornbækhaus, a five-story brick building of nearly three hundred one-, two-, and three-bedroom apartments ringing an immense courtyard. Just a mile north of where Juhl grew up, Hornbækhaus was a world away. But Juhl would have known its legacy; Fisker trained his students in the study of housing, assigning them to research Copenhagen's residential architecture. Some of this research, published in a series of illustrated articles in the Danish magazine *Arkitekten*, revealed the significance of Copenhagen building codes, which kept new construction lower than the city's modest church spires, promoting horizontal rather than vertical density.[12] New apartment complexes like Fisker's had large footprints, often a full city block, but were never more than five stories tall. Structures slender in depth encircled large, central courtyards, allowing light and air into the apartments. Outfitted with advanced amenities like central heating and hot water, the apartments offered modern comforts but little space. Their floor plans prioritized residents' access to outdoor communal space, where Juhl's large Chieftain might have fit more easily than in one of the small apartments. Juhl's own house also prioritized access to the outdoors, with nearly every room opening onto the grassy garden, but inside, the Chieftain could fit comfortably. Though hardly grand, his house offered roomy living areas and a home office connected by an art-filled sitting area, where the Chieftain sat next to a modern fireplace with a brick hearth protruding into the room like an area rug (fig. 1.2). The image of open space strikes a sharp contrast with the dwelling reality of most Copenhageners at the time.

Though the Chieftain's price tag and designer status made it an unlikely presence in the new apartment blocks, oversize furniture was not unusual. Many residents sought to reproduce their old interiors, nestling, for instance, a high-backed armchair between an upright piano and a grandfather clock (fig. 1.3). Such items made the new apartments feel like home. Juhl's contemporaries, however, were busy conceiving furniture specifically for these compact living quarters. They imagined small, handy pieces that would take up little space—like a wall-mounted vanity or a dining table that folded down from the wall like a Murphy bed (fig. 1.4a)—and, to get by with fewer pieces, multipurpose furnishings called *forvandlingsmøbler*—a storage unit that doubled as a minibar or a two-seat sofa that converted into a daybed (fig. 1.4b).[13] As in other Nordic countries during the period, pamphlets on interior organization circulated alongside building codes specifying building heights, door widths, and stair inclines. Beginning in 1955, Denmark's Housing Ministry had to approve furniture layout plans as well as architectural ones for builders to receive government loans for residential buildings.[14] While apartment dwellers may have preferred roomy armchairs, Juhl and his classmates were trained to anticipate small, handy chairs and other furnishings scaled to the new smaller spaces.

Figure 1.2 Finn Juhl seated in Chieftain at home, ca. 1950s. DesignMuseum
Danmark. Photographer unknown.

Figure 1.3 Snapshot from a Danish family album, ca. 1940s. The Royal Library. Photographer unknown.

Figure 1.4a Helge Vestergaard Jensen (designer), Thysen Nielsen (fabricator), folding table, 1955. Teak.

Figure 1.4b Hans Olsen (designer), V. Birksholm (fabricator), settee sleeper, 1955. Teak and fabric.

The Chieftain snubbed the period mandate to design for the new realities of urban dwelling. Its size made it unfit for the compact apartments sprouting up around Copenhagen, causing some of Juhl's peers to view it as elitist. And yet, while its floating structure was thoroughly modern, its size honored the mainstream popularity of antique-style armchairs.

Studying Furniture

If the Chieftain was a rebuttal to the "small handy chairs" that were the norm among Juhl's colleagues, Wegner's Round Chair—the Chair, as it is known—was an affirmation. "The pure and simple design of the armchair was completely unencumbered by artistic mannerisms," wrote one critic.[15] Its spare wood frame and cane seat make it light enough to lift and carry with one hand. That the chair back doubles as an informal handle means it is easy to move around a room, from desk to dining table to sitting area. Handy, indeed. Nearly twenty-five inches wide, the Chair is hardly slight—"your rear end needs room," Wegner supposedly said—but at two-thirds the width of the Chieftain, it looks the part of the small chairs to which Juhl was responding.[16]

When Wegner designed his Chair, he had in mind a specific fabricator—cabinetmaker Johannes Hansen. By 1949, when Hansen's workshop made the Chair, the two men had been working together for close to a decade. (Juhl had a similarly lengthy relationship with cabinetmaker Niels Vodder, who made the Chieftain.) But Hansen was only one of several makers with whom Wegner worked. He had designed small lines and one-offs for various Danish manufacturers: among others, modular office furnishings for Aarhus-based Planmøbler; a riff on a nineteenth-century

Chinese chair included in a line of bentwood furniture produced by Fritz Hansen, one of Denmark's largest manufacturers; and a rocking chair and child's table-and-chair set for FDB Møbler, a cooperative established in 1942 to offer affordable modern furnishings. Wegner had experience with fabricators working in a range of settings, from the small scale of the workshop to the larger, partially industrialized scale of the factory. But he wanted Hansen to make the Round Chair because Hansen was a cabinetmaker and the Chair was an exercise in masterful joinery.

This is most evident in the Chair's top rail, where a pronounced W-shaped finger joint connects the vertical face of the chair back to the arms. Maximizing the surface area of the connection makes the chair back strong, but the functional joint also provides a decorative element as elegant as inlay (fig. 1.5). Wegner devised the novel joint himself. He had trained as a joiner but, like Juhl, made his living as a designer, not a maker, running a drawing office rather than a workshop. Yet even though Wegner and Juhl did the same work, they were known by different titles: Juhl was an *arkitekt*, and Wegner was not. In midcentury Denmark, when "designer" was not yet part of common parlance, designations like cabinetmaker (*snedker*) and *arkitekt*, conferred by education, not practice, were meaningful as social markers. The prestigious title of *arkitekt*— reserved exclusively for graduates of the Royal Danish Academy of Fine Arts, School of Architecture, the nation's most selective school—was proudly worn by graduates, even those who did not go on to practice. And it remained an indicator of professional orientation; even if Juhl eschewed aspects of what he had learned during his training under Fisker, those lessons served as anchors for his subsequent career. The same was true for Wegner.

In 1930, when Juhl started at the Royal Academy, Wegner, two years

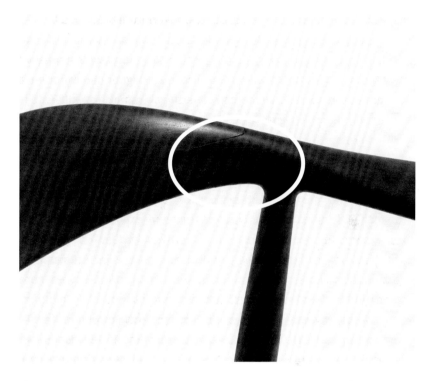

Figure 1.5 Hans Wegner (designer), Johannes Hansen (fabricator), Round Chair (detail show-ing joinery), 1949. Courtesy of Rago/Wright.

his junior, was already well into an apprenticeship as a cabinetmaker. The training was demanding but not rarefied; there were cabinetmakers in towns and cities across Denmark and, thus, many places to learn the craft. Wegner began his education as an apprentice to Hermann Frie-drich Nicolaus Stahlberg, a cabinetmaker in his hometown of Tønder, a small city two hundred miles southeast of Copenhagen. He finished his training in 1931 but stayed on as a journeyman for three more years before leaving for Copenhagen, joining the thousands of Danes newly arrived in the capital. It was not financial ruin that brought him there but military service, and when he completed it he enrolled in Kunsthåndvaerkersko-lens Snedkerdagskole (Cabinetmaker Day School at the School of Arts and Crafts; now Danmarks Designskole, or Danish Design School). That Wegner, who already had six years' experience as a cabinetmaker, sought more schooling speaks as much to his dedication to his craft as it does to the status of cabinetmaking in Copenhagen, where it was perceived less as a trade than a profession.

The Cabinetmaker Day School offered lessons in carving and marque-try, which Wegner had learned in Stahlberg's workshop, and drawing, which he had recently studied during a ten-week course at Teknologisk Institut (Danish Technological Institute). The Day School, sponsored by Kunstindustrimuseet (Museum of Industrial Art; now DesignMuseum Danmark) and housed within the same building, offered an education rooted in the museum's collection, deliberately assembled to present students with a wide array of contemporary and historical designs. This was not Wegner's first experience learning from museum collections; as a boy, he had often visited the newly built art museum in Tønder and used its holdings as inspiration for small, carved wooden sculptures. While the Tønder museum was dedicated to Nordic art, the Museum of Industrial Art's collection, with its emphasis on furniture and other applied arts, had far more geographical scope. It was strongest in European design and included, for instance, art nouveau furnishings from Siegfried Bing's exhibition at the 1900 world's fair in Paris, a Wiener Werkstätte piece by Josef Hoffmann, and an array of modern Dutch furniture. But it was lim-ited neither to European design nor to modernism. For example, shortly after Wegner enrolled at the school in 1936, the museum acquired a

Chinese chair dated to the seventeenth or eighteenth century. It was a standout in the collection, unique in that it was constructed without nails, screws, or glue. Wegner and his classmates studied objects like it in numerous exercises, including one in which they were asked to reverse-engineer an object's construction. This provided an opportunity not only to develop their drawing skills but to study and learn from design history. Wegner took the lesson to heart. He was particularly captivated by a Chippendale chair, which appears in a number of his school assignments, and after graduation, he continued to refer to the museum's collection. The Chinese chair, in particular, along with another chair of Chinese origin illustrated in a 1932 book by Wilhelm Wanscher, served as the foundation for a number of his own designs, including the Round Chair.[17]

In addition to teaching design history, the Cabinetmaker Day School was a place to acquire a professional network. Wegner trained under the promising young designer Orla (O.) Mølgaard-Nielsen—later instructors included Aksel Bender Madsen and Peter Hvidt—and alongside peers, like Børge Mogensen, who would soon become giants of Danish furniture. The school afforded Wegner an opportunity to learn from their expertise and, equally importantly, to make connections that would prove crucial when he launched his postgraduate career. It was Mølgaard-Nielsen who recommended Wegner to Johannes Hansen as a potential collaborator, and Mogensen who, as design director of FDB Møbler, invited him to design children's furniture for the company. While Wegner was widely recognized and admired for his virtuosity (in 1944, he cut and set three thousand individual pieces of intarsia for an ornate aquatic scene, teeming with flora and fish, on the interior door of an otherwise modest-seeming desk), it was connections as well as skill that positioned him to receive these opportunities. The school furnished students like Wegner with entry to a community of Copenhagen-based craftsmen who referred to those beyond their ranks as "outsiders."[18]

The Round Chair was an homage to that community. It was, Wegner said, "designed for Danish craftsmen."[19] But it might be more accurate to say that it was designed for, and because of, Copenhagen cabinetmakers. After designing his Chinese chair for Fritz Hansen, Wegner made his first sketches toward the Chair. In these, he removed the Chinese chair's central vertical support for the backrest, a feature that would become the Chair's hallmark (fig. 1.6). The process links the design not only to specific furniture pieces from the past, but also to a way of forging new designs through careful engagement with historical ones—a lesson Wegner learned at the Cabinetmaker Day School.[20] After he further developed the design for the Chair, it was a Copenhagen cabinetmaker who fabricated it. Though it's conceivable that Wegner intended the Chair as a tribute to Stahlberg, his first mentor, and other tradesmen in small towns and cities across the country, his experiences in Copenhagen launched its conception and development. If the Chair was "designed for Danish craftsmen," that is, "Danish" may designate less a trade circumscribed by national borders than a Copenhagen-based community constituted by particular individuals and institutions.

The Royal Academy's School of Architecture, Juhl's alma mater, was also central to this community. Indeed, its furniture department is often cited as the point of origin for Danish design's postwar rise. Wegner's teacher Mølgaard-Nielsen had trained there at roughly the same time as Juhl, but while Juhl was studying housing with Kay Fisker, Mølgaard-Nielsen was studying under Kaare Klint, in the furniture department Klint had founded in 1924. Klint would describe his pedagogy as based upon methodical, rational study. In a magazine article

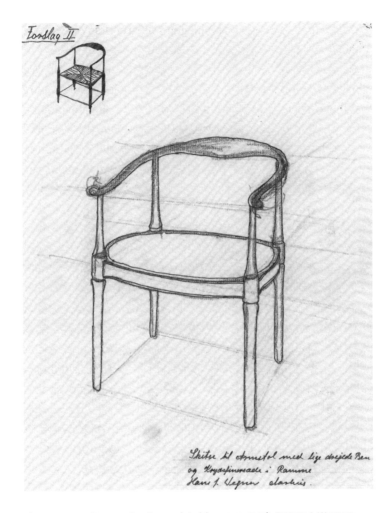

Figure 1.6 Hans Wegner, drawing, undated (ca. 1945–1949). © Hans J. Wegners Tegnestue I/S.

from 1930, one of his rare pieces of published writing, he enumerated its underlying tenets: "Measurement as the preliminary study for further production—human measurements and movements—measurements of objects—constructive relationships in connection with conditions for use—methods of collection, treatment of material, aesthetic considerations, common work."[21] This functionalist approach, which a Royal Academy colleague described as "work as zealous as a scientist's," involved tireless studies of people as well as common objects like dishware and clothing.[22] A shelving system was never to extend higher than a man of average height could reach, a credenza's drawers never to be deeper than the diameter of an average dinner plate. Klint's research was intended to prepare students to design for the realities of modern life, and it also informed his own practice. He deployed his system of measurement to inform assumptions about the bodies, possessions, and preferences of an object's eventual users, as when he scaled the design of a sideboard to store a complete table service for twelve. In his pedagogy and in his furniture (frequently based on measurements and drawings made by current and former students), his approach to design centered on an imagined user. While his colleagues in the architecture department researched arrangements of furniture to suit modern dwelling spaces, Klint and his students sought to design furniture scientifically suited to those who inhabited them.

Like the instructors at the Cabinetmaker Day School, Klint required his students to study historical designs. And just as he borrowed their measuring work, so too did he borrow this research. When a Copenhagen auction house sold a Shaker rocking chair in 1927, Klint sent two of his students to make drawings of it, and then commissioned Rud. Rasmussens Snedkerier, a cabinetmaking company with whom he frequently worked, to fabricate a replica with only minor variations, such as a flat rather than curved top rail. (The cabinetmaker then displayed the copy in its shop window with a sign that read, "Designed by Kaare Klint.") Usually, though, Klint brought his students to the Museum of Industrial Art, only half a mile from their campus, so that they too could study the objects in its collection and make use of the books in its library. While there, students sat in chairs and at tables designed by their teacher, who in 1926 had collaborated on a redesign of the building, formerly a hospital, in which the museum and the Cabinetmaker Day School were housed. Surrounded by their teacher's designs, they were instructed to root their work in historical furniture. These shared study spaces, reference collections, and pedagogical approaches primed the students in the furniture department at the Royal Academy's School of Architecture and the Cabinetmaker Day School for collaboration.

Exhibiting Danish Design

In 1927 a small group of Copenhagen cabinetmakers organized Snedkerlaugets Udstilling (the Cabinetmakers Guild Exhibition) in the hopes of reviving their trade. "The craft of cabinetmaking is struggling to hold its own against the steadily growing industrial furniture production," explained one critic.[23] With so much inexpensive furniture on the domestic market, much of it imported from abroad, business was bad. The exhibition was to be a place where cabinetmakers could showcase new designs and, more importantly, sell them. In terms of both visitors and sales, it exceeded expectations. More than twenty thousand people visited, and sales were brisk. Before the inaugural exhibition closed, the cabinetmakers were already planning one for the following year. They held that exhibition in the autumn of 1928 and another each year after that, even during the war, until 1966. The initial orientation toward sales remained throughout the forty-year run insofar as every exhibited piece of furniture was available for purchase. So too did the goal of fostering interest in good and beautiful handmade furniture by satisfying the specific wishes and tastes of customers, with visitors encouraged to custom order the furnishings they saw.[24] To ensure their pieces were relevant for contemporary living conditions, some cabinetmakers invited the furniture *arkitekts* who studied those conditions to collaborate on new designs.[25] It was there, at the 1949 Cabinetmakers Exhibition, that Juhl and Wegner premiered the Chieftain and the Chair (figs. 1.1 and 1.7).

By the time the two chairs debuted, the Cabinetmakers Exhibition had become a two-week cultural event, attracting close to thirty thousand visitors each year. Most were Danes, but it also drew guests from abroad, some from nearby Sweden and Norway, others from further afield, including the United States, South Africa, and Italy. As Bent Salicath, an *arkitekt* and managing director of the professional organization Landsforeningen Dansk Kunsthaandværk (the Danish Society of Arts and Crafts and Industrial Design), wrote in an unpublished, midcentury survey of Danish industrial design, the exhibitions began as an effort to deal with an unemployment crisis in the cabinetmaking trade, but over time the annual event transformed the furniture industry and became a "cultural achievement of vital importance."[26]

Already at the first exhibition, a few cabinetmakers collaborated with furniture *arkitekts* to fabricate pieces conceived by the *arkitekts*. Though such collaborations were met with internal resistance from some Cabinetmakers Guild members into the early 1930s, many others viewed

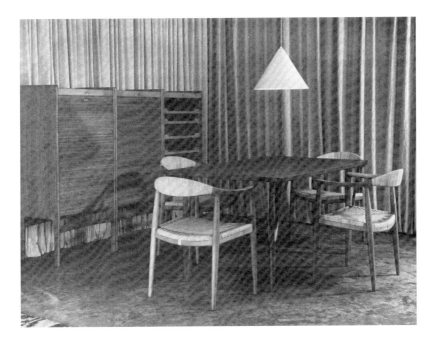

Figure 1.7 Johannes Hansen display featuring furniture designed by Hans Wegner, Cabinet-makers Guild Exhibition, 1949.

them as an opportunity to refresh their staid craft, invigorating it with the functionalist approach to design propagated by Klint's students at the Royal Academy. Over time, some cabinetmakers formalized their partnerships, maintaining ongoing collaborations with specific design-ers. Niels Vodder, for example, worked year after year with Juhl, and Johannes Hansen did the same with Wegner. The Cabinetmakers Guild fostered these relationships by staging competitions, beginning in 1933, in which *arkitekts* were invited to design furnishings for an interior with a specific profile, like a one-bedroom apartment of specified dimensions

(1942) or a weekend cottage with a living room, bedroom, and terrace (1958). The winning entries to the spring competition would be selected by cabinetmakers for fabrication over the summer and display in the fall. Though the Cabinetmakers Exhibition was open to the public for only two weeks, *arkitekts* and cabinetmakers were involved in related activities for nearly half the year.

In addition to structuring regular dialogue among Copenhagen's *arkitekts* and cabinetmakers, the competition served as the entry point for participation in the annual exhibition and, by extension, the design community. If a designer had never before shown at the Cabinetmakers Exhibition, the drawings entered in the spring competition had not only to be selected by a cabinetmaker but also to be approved by a member of the exhibition's organizing committee, thus granting guild leaders a measure of control over the kinds of work displayed at the annual showcase.[27] In the fall, when the furniture premiered, the designs would again be judged, now as furnished spaces rather than two-dimensional plans, permitting guild leaders an opportunity to shape the direction of new design by pointing the public's attention to certain pieces. (Juhl's Chieftain, and the double Chieftain, coffee table, and dining set that accompanied it at the 1949 exhibition, won first prize that year.) As exemplified by Kaare Klint's work with Rud. Rasmussen on the Shaker-inspired rocking chair, partnerships between *arkitekts* and cabinetmakers also took place outside the exhibitions. But with participation carefully overseen, the exhibitions controlled access to a wider audience and, in the words of Nils Borén, for a time the chairman of the Cabinetmakers Guild's exhibition committee, cultivated a sense of "solidarity" among those admitted.[28]

By the late 1930s, the guild had begun renting space for the exhibitions in the Museum of Industrial Art, solidifying that institution, where students from the Cabinetmaker Day School and the furniture department at the Royal Academy also studied, as the spatial center of Copenhagen's design community. The Klint-designed interiors were reconfigured for the show. Parquet panels covered the oversize granite floor tiles, and temporary walls split the large, open galleries into a series of small rooms—"little scenes," one critic called them—each featuring a different cabinetmaker.[29] These scenes were often playful, outfitted not only with furniture but with artwork, textiles, and other objects to give the impression of a lived interior. Young women hired to work the exhibition led tours, inviting visitors to sit on a sofa or demonstrating a bar cart's storage capacity.[30] Though furniture continued to be sold—even before the 1945 fair opened, an American tourist bought every single piece Juhl had designed for Niels Vodder's display—by the end of World War II, the Cabinetmakers Exhibition was no longer first and foremost a retail endeavor. New designs could be exhibited with little pressure or even expectation to sell. Displays sometimes even included works in progress rather than finished designs. Wegner's Chair, for example, was shown with its back wrapped in cane because, as the story goes, he had not yet perfected the signature finger joint. With increased emphasis on experimentation, the exhibitions came to be known by some as "laboratories of innovation," and by the late 1950s, the competition guidelines were specifically revised to reward "experimental work on design."[31]

This emphasis may have prompted some new ideas, such as Wegner's collaboration with a polio researcher to design a chair with optimal lumbar support. But experimentation had its limits. In 1950, when A. J. Iversen presented a clear table made of plastic, it was lambasted by reviewers, who saw a cabinetmaker forgetting that he was a carpenter, and thus betraying his craft.[32] Far more celebrated was the sideboard Kaare Klint designed, using his students' research, to neatly fit china, glasses, flatware, and table linens belonging to a so-called typical family of four. As *arkitekt* Willy Hansen explained in his review of the 1930 exhibition, where the sideboard debuted, Klint "has analyzed and measured the many different factors and objects—dimensions, worked out on the basis of the proportions of the human body and its movements, measurement of the paper, china, glasses, linen, clothes, etc. etc.— which determine the form of a piece of furniture." Hansen characterized this approach, which Klint taught to his students at the Royal Academy, as the "scientific analysis of the fundamentals of furniture design."[33] (The design was so influential that, twenty years later, *New York Times* columnist Betty Pepis mentioned it in one of the paper's first articles on Danish design.[34]) But Klint's analysis was flawed in its hypothesis; its foundational premise of a "typical" family, and the measuring technique deployed to design for it, oversimplified the varied reality of human body types and abilities. And while its modular system was based upon measurements of affordable items like a china set from the popular department store Magasin du Nord, the sideboard itself was custom, with a price tag to match. Though Juhl and others imagined a trickle-down effect in which design ideas debuted at the exhibition would eventually make their way into affordable, mass-produced furniture, one critic hit the mark when he described the furniture on display as "new—and often expensive—experiments."[35]

The paradox of Klint's custom-made, modular sideboard speaks to an underlying truth about the purpose of the Cabinetmakers Exhibition. Though the furniture shown might go on to spark new trends, the specific designs would not themselves transform modern living for the masses.

Neither the Chieftain nor the smaller, handier Chair would furnish the apartments in Hornbækhaus. The cabinetmakers cast this as a virtue. In a context of increasingly industrialized production, organized to make uniform goods and sell them to as many people as possible, they were uniquely positioned to cultivate "personal direct cooperation with the public," furnishing "customers with the special desires and tastes of their homes, irrespective of the prevailing fashion of the moment."[36] Small-scale production meant they could offer made-to-order pieces; customers could, for example, select the type of wood from which a chair would be made, or the fabric used to upholster it—albeit at higher prices.

This model, however, also provoked criticism. Some described the designs shown at the Cabinetmakers Exhibitions as "artful curiosities," whimsical frivolities with little everyday relevance.[37] Others, like designer and critic Poul Henningsen (better known as PH), went further, condemning the exhibitions as elitist. Why were *arkitekts* and cabinetmakers devoting their time and attention to expensive experiments rather than the practical needs of a broader public? Defenders of the exhibition argued that even if the objects presented were not available to all, the displays gave shape to the Danish furniture industry and would influence what was made and sold elsewhere.[38]

These debates were important both because of their content, which put pressure on *arkitekts* and cabinetmakers to interrogate and defend their practices and, especially, because they took place in the public sphere, on the pages of popular newspapers. Since at least the nineteenth century, Danish theorists and industry members had been reflecting on the character and purpose of furniture and other applied arts, but these debates typically happened behind closed office doors or in the pages of specialist journals like *Tidsskrift for Kunstindustri* (Journal for the Applied Arts). As annual, public events, the Cabinetmakers Exhibitions expanded the conversation about the role and purpose of modern furniture and, in the process, helped to define the field.

This was particularly clear in the publications and pamphlets that accompanied the exhibitions. In 1951, for example, exhibition organizers published *Dansk Møbelkunst* (Danish Furniture Art), a book commemorating the twenty-fifth anniversary of the Cabinetmakers Exhibition. While the title suggests an overview of the country's design scene, the book's pages describe the history of the exhibition, as though it alone constituted Danish furniture art. Beyond creating a space for a close-knit group of designers and makers educated and based in Copenhagen to present new designs, the Cabinetmakers Exhibitions positioned their work as Danish design itself. Over the course of the 1950s, during which exhibition pamphlets began to be printed in English as well as Danish, the dissonance between the narratives' focus on a limited group of cabinetmakers and *arkitekts* and the titles' claims to represent national design (e.g., *Exhibition of Modern Danish Hand-made Furniture*, 1960) would be resolved as the two came to be seen as interchangeable. Especially abroad, the design community forged by the Cabinetmaker Day School, the Royal Academy's School of Architecture, and the Cabinetmakers Exhibitions would define Danish design for a generation.

This definition would take root internationally as soon as the Chieftain and the Chair arrived on American shores. They made their first appearance in *Interiors*, a trade magazine for interior designers, architects, and industrial designers, in an article titled "Danish Furniture: Old Hands Give Shape to New Ideas." It focused exclusively on furniture exhibited at the 1949 Cabinetmakers Exhibition and, based on what was shown there, generalized about the field of Danish design. "Danish armchairs as a rule are not overstuffed or even completely upholstered," the article explained, "but made with light frames and provided with cushions."[39] As two of the twelve designs pictured, what the magazine called Juhl's "piece" and Wegner's "desk chair" modeled this new definition.[40]

: : :

The year after he designed the Chieftain, Juhl wrote that had he trained as a cabinetmaker, he "would never have dared to design my furniture but would have been thinking about tariffs and common carpentry joints."[41] He was proud of his lack of formal training, often insisting that as a furniture designer, he was "completely self-taught."[42] Positioning himself as a free thinker—more an artist driven by inspiration than a trained professional steeped in industry standards—Juhl revealed his understanding of the ways in which education governs design by structuring patterns of thought. During the interwar period, the Cabinetmaker Day School and the furniture department at the Royal Academy trained young cabinetmakers and *arkitekts* in a series of approaches, including historical and measurement-based research, that would ground their subsequent design work, even the work of those, like Juhl, who sought to rebel against them.

Just as importantly, these institutions produced a community of practitioners who shared references and techniques, as well as physical workspaces. This Copenhagen-based community was shaped by specific national conditions and their material consequences, like the economic crisis that caused tens of thousands to leave rural areas for the city. And it was reinforced by the Cabinetmakers Exhibitions, whose annual calendar of spring competition and autumn exhibition kept the community's members in conversation with one another, binding their work and their reputations. By putting new furniture on display for a public, the Cabinetmakers Exhibitions gave legible form to the notion of "Danish design," such that it came to refer, not to a diverse and dispersed industry, but to one particular segment where craftsmanship was king.

Made in Denmark

When the Chieftain and the Chair premiered at the 1949 Cabinetmakers Exhibition in Copenhagen, both were eclipsed in the press by another star: the United States. One Swedish writer observed that "American-inspired curved wooden structures made their mark on the exhibition," shaping its "experimental spirit."[1] Another attributed the evident vogue for plywood to prize-winning designs from the recent International Low-Cost Furniture Competition at the Museum of Modern Art (MoMA) in New York, to which Wegner had submitted designs.[2] (Though the competition was international in scope—three thousand entries from thirty-one countries—more than half of the winners were American, and every member of the selection committee was based in the US.) Danish *arkitekts* and cabinetmakers were borrowing from American trends.

The potential American audience for Danish furniture was also noted. Danish newspapers reported that MoMA had recently exhibited and then purchased two of Juhl's designs, and speculated that this would help ripen the US market for Danish design.[3] One paper excitedly observed that American journalists and tourists had been among the first visitors to the Cabinetmakers Exhibition, and reported on a young American who had skipped her Danish-language class to attend but made up for it by leaving with a long list of names and addresses of where to buy Danish furniture—as though exchanging one demonstration of commitment to Danish culture for another.[4] Press accounts thus make clear that when the Chieftain and the Chair debuted, they entered into a Copenhagen design world preoccupied with the United States and the possibilities of expanding exports.

This interest had been building for years, if not decades. A government-sponsored touring exhibition, *Danish National Exhibition of Paintings, Sculpture, Arts, and Crafts* (including tables, chairs, and sideboards "showing Dutch and English influence"), had premiered at the Brooklyn Museum in 1927, and following the 1939 world's fair in New York, a retail exhibition that included Danish furniture had traveled to department stores across the US.[5] But members of Copenhagen's design community approached the project with new vigor after the war; at a time when Europe's markets showed persistent volatility, America's expanding economy presented a ripe site for industry growth.

The Chieftain and the Chair would do more than just ride the wave of export. They would serve as ambassadors, actively contributing to the reputation of Danish design overseas and advancing the relationship between the Danish and American furniture industries. In the process, the chairs themselves were transformed. Juhl would redesign the Chieftain's joinery to accommodate industrial manufacture by an American company, and Johannes Hansen, the Chair's maker, would reorganize his workshop's systems of production to meet American demand. Individual efforts to make the designs viable on the American market were bolstered by government support, particularly in the form of wood subsidies. Danish design, as evidenced by these export-oriented reconfigurations of objects and infrastructures, was literally made for America.

Designing for Americans

When Edgar Kaufmann Jr., director of the industrial design department at the Museum of Modern Art in New York, introduced Finn Juhl to the readers of *Interiors* in a 1948 profile, he called Juhl a "master chair designer" working in the tradition of "Sheraton, Hepplewhite, Chippendale, and their followers, whose best works are peerless."[6] Launched by this enthusiastic endorsement, Juhl's star would continue to rise over the next few years. He received work in the United States and, with it, more visibility among American design professionals, tastemakers, and popular audiences. In 1950 he won the commission to design the Trusteeship Council chamber at the United Nations headquarters in New York, joining a high-profile team of architects that included Le Corbusier and Oscar Niemeyer.[7] (Denmark donated the chamber in exchange for the right to design it, and Juhl was selected by a committee made up of representatives from his alma mater, the Royal Danish Academy of Fine Arts.) Later that year, Kaufmann invited him to design the 1951 installments of *Good Design*, a program celebrating contemporary design that included two exhibitions at Chicago's Merchandise Mart and one at the Museum of Modern Art each year between 1950 and 1955. (Wegner's Chair was among the objects exhibited in 1951, though Juhl had no hand in selecting it.[8]) Also in 1951, Juhl began designing a line of modern furnishings for Baker, a popular American furniture manufacturer based in Grand Rapids, Michigan.

While the UN and *Good Design* projects were prestigious commissions within the design field, the Baker collaboration offered a unique opportunity to reach a popular audience by designing for retail. Toward that end, Juhl resurrected and reworked a number of pieces he had designed for cabinetmaker Neils Vodder in the 1940s. But the furniture never really found a broader market. It had its best season in 1956, when General Motors chose the line to outfit its new Technical Center outside Detroit, including the private office of Harley Earl, its vice president in charge of styling.[9] Baker used pictures of the GM installations to drum up interest in the designs, previously marketed for home use, as office furnishings. This was one of several rebrands the company tried over the course of its six-year partnership with Juhl—none of which capitalized on the furniture as Danish.

The collaboration between Baker and Juhl began with the Chieftain. Hollis Baker, the furniture company's chairman, was so taken with the chair, after seeing it illustrated in a 1950 *Interiors* article about the 1949 Cabinetmakers Exhibition where it had premiered, that he adjusted the itinerary of his upcoming European tour to include a stop in Copenhagen. While there in June, he invited a skeptical Juhl to visit the Baker factory, offering an all-expense-paid trip plus $1,000 for two weeks' lost earnings (at the time, roughly a quarter of the average American family's annual income). Juhl accepted. In Grand Rapids three months later, he was impressed with what he saw. The company's use of high-quality woods and veneers, and its practice of hand-finishing each mass-produced piece, made a particularly strong impression. The American firm and the Danish designer spent the next nine months exchanging and marking up sketches and drawings. Baker premiered the line at an industry buyer's market in June 1951, calling it "Baker Modern."

This, at least, was the story told to retailers in the company news-letter, the *Baker Bugle*. Written as promotion, it offers less insight into how the collaboration came about than into how the company wanted to sell itself and its new line. The account presents Baker as a thriving company (paying Juhl's way, with a generous stipend) committed to high-quality mass production and actively engaged in the design pro-cess. Hollis Baker comes off as a man possessing both good taste and the power of persuasion. The Chieftain, meanwhile, having prompted the chairman to recruit Juhl, is positioned as the piece that launched the line—design so good it sold itself.

Though the name Baker Modern suggests no regional affiliation, Juhl's designs were realized with the help of Danish production. Cabinetmaker Niels Vodder fabricated every one of the samples Baker showed at the 1951 industry buyer's market, during which American department and furniture store representatives selected items to stock their showrooms for the coming season. This was only one of the ways in which Juhl's work with Vodder shaped the collection.

The Baker collaboration gave Juhl an opportunity to play with new, synthetic materials largely unavailable in Denmark, but the initial, fifteen-piece line hewed to his usual work in wood. Apart from a wood-frame coffee table topped with a piece of Formica that bent over the edge of the frame and hung halfway down the side, the designs were shaped significantly by ones he had initially conceived for Vodder. For example, the Baker dining table featured contrasting woods—a soft-edged oval of walnut set into sycamore so blond it was almost white—echoing the concept, though not the shape or structure, of the dining table Juhl had shown alongside the Chieftain in 1949. An upholstered walnut dining chair structurally replicated one he had designed for Vodder (plates 4 and 5). And a wall-mounted shelving unit modified a design shown at the 1948 Cabinetmakers Exhibition to accommodate the standard sixteen-inch spacing of wall studs in American houses.

A change to nonmetric dimensions was one of numerous adjustments Juhl made to sell his furniture in the United States. Others involved materials. Three domestically grown woods—English sycamore, rock maple, and walnut—were used for Baker Modern. Pieces made of walnut, one of the most popular furniture woods in midcentury America, made up the bulk of the collection. So, for example, while the Vodder shelving unit had been made of maple, the Baker one was available in white sycamore or walnut, but *not* in maple, as if to distinguish it from its Danish predecessor. Juhl also used other American-manufactured materials, like synthetic upholstery fabrics, rather than the natural-fiber textiles used in Denmark.

Given Juhl's nationality and the rootedness of so many of the American pieces in designs first realized in Denmark, Baker could easily have sold his designs as Danish. Doing so would have been consistent with other of the company's lines, like "Far East," referencing China, and "Palladian," evoking France and Italy. But in this case, the first time Baker commissioned an external designer to conceive a line instead of relying on in-house designers, it avoided such associations, promoting the furniture as made for Americans in America. The *Baker Bugle* lauded the line as "suitable in design and feeling for our American use," and the first page of a pamphlet on the collaboration read "For American Manufacture," written in Juhl's distinctive hand.[10] Baker insisted that the company had hired Juhl to design its modern line simply because he was "the best."[11] But the best did not translate into sales.

In the first few years after the line's launch, the American manufacturer rebranded Baker Modern a number of times, trying out different marketing approaches. First, Baker changed the name to "Finn Juhl," a switch that capitalized on the growing celebrity of designers in postwar America: beginning with its first issue in 1953, *Playboy* featured architects and designers like Ludwig Mies van der Rohe and Frank Lloyd Wright in its pages; also in 1953, *Life* highlighted designer Florence Knoll and her manufacturer husband Hans in an article about their modern furniture company, Knoll Associates; and the NBC program *Home* introduced Charles and Ray Eames to viewers in 1956, with the host acknowledging that by that point, "Charles Eames has become almost a household word."[12] Though Juhl was a foreigner and Baker a committedly American company, attaching the designer's name to the line was an attempt to capitalize on this trend, particularly as Juhl's fame grew with the opening of the UN building in 1952. In 1954 the Chieftain was added to the Finn Juhl line, albeit without the Chieftain name—it was distinguished from the line's other chairs only by a model number (440½). Nonetheless, the Baker Chieftain received pride of place in the collection, and appeared as the sole illustrated object in a short run of print ads for it.

As with many of his other designs for Baker, Juhl modified the Chieftain's design, if only slightly. In place of the teak Vodder had used, the Baker chair was made of American walnut. (This was a deliberate choice; Baker imported teak for other furniture lines.) To make factory production easier, Juhl suggested replacing the vertical step joint at the chair's horn with a horizontally affixed cap (fig. 2.1a–b).[13] While the company would deploy this modification when it rereleased the Chieftain in the 1990s, the 1950s version kept the original step joint but elongated it. The Baker Chieftain was nearly identical to a Vodder-made one then touring the United States as part of a large (and lauded) exhibition of Scandi-

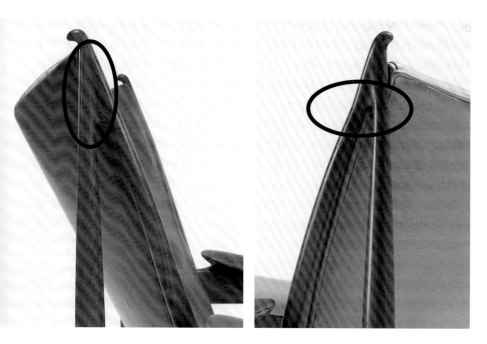

Figure 2.1a Finn Juhl (designer), Niels Vodder (fabricator), Chieftain Chair (detail showing stepped joint), 1950s. Courtesy of Rago/Wright. **Figure 2.1b** Finn Juhl (designer), Baker (fabricator), Chieftain Chair (detail showing capped horn), 1990s. Courtesy of Rago/Wright.

navian design. The Chieftain was, in many ways, Baker's most Danish design yet, but still the company did not capitalize on the connection.

It was only at the end of the collaboration, after Baker had already begun dropping Juhl's designs from production, that it finally pivoted to a marketing strategy foregrounding Juhl's regional affiliation. In 1956 the company recast the dispersed set of global allusions associated with its lines as part of a "One World" branding concept, marketing "Finn Juhl designs from Scandinavia" alongside an array of globally sourced materials: "handwoven silk from Thailand, teak from Burma," and "brasses from Italy, granite from Norway, hardware from India, choice walnut and cherry from France, unusual cabinet woods from South America, onyx from Portugal and South Africa, and pure raw silk from Japan."[14] Juhl's inclusion on this list suggests that by then Baker had begun to think of him less as a contributing designer than as a useful imported resource.

Before the Baker collaboration premiered, when some of Juhl's designs, imported from Denmark, were displayed in the window of a New York department store, *Interiors* reported that "all the more discriminating interior designers, manufacturers, distributors, furniture buyers, retailers and lovers of fine furniture in the country were peering with craned necks toward the same watery juncture of the Cattegat, the Baltic and the misty North Sea."[15] The Danish press would later assert that this attention was due to the furniture's "outstanding quality, in design as well as in craftsmanship," and would attribute the industry's success abroad particularly to Juhl, Wegner, and two other designers (Børge Mogensen and Jacob Kjær).[16] But Juhl's failed collaboration with Baker makes clear that good design alone was not enough to turn American heads. Even if Juhl was, as Baker claimed, "the best," Danish design's growing success in the United States depended on a number of other factors having to do with the logistics and practicality of fabrication and export.

Fabricating for Americans

Hollis Baker was one of many American design professionals to admire the furniture featured in *Interiors*'s article about the 1949 Cabinetmakers Exhibition. When Raymond Loewy, an industrial designer famous for products like the Lincoln Continental and the packaging for Lucky Strike cigarettes, saw the spread, he wrote to the magazine asking for more information about Wegner's Round Chair and how he could buy one.[17] American manufacturers were similarly interested and inquired about licensing the design for stateside production. (Wegner turned them down.) A group of Chicagoans, who wished to use the Chair in their members-only club, tried to place an order. As interest grew, the Chair became a test case for determining how Danish production could be restructured to suit the scale of the American market.

When the orders began rolling in, Johannes Hansen was unprepared. The cabinetmaker had not yet sold the four Round Chairs fabricated for the Cabinetmakers Exhibition, and he was happy to offer them to American buyers. But when the Chicagoans called, they didn't want just four chairs. They wanted four hundred. Hansen couldn't fill the order. Like most cabinetmakers, his operation was small. He had only five craftsmen in his workshop, too few to make so many chairs in any reasonable time frame. And then there was the matter of credit: Hansen would need a down payment to secure the materials and labor needed for so large an order, while Americans were accustomed to a forty-day grace period between placing an order and the first payment coming due.[18]

Popularizing Danish design in the United States, as Hansen's dilemma demonstrates, required innovation in production as well as design. The problem was not a new one: after the 1939 New York World's Fair, the Danish exhibition that toured American department stores highlighted designs by manufacturer Fritz Hansen because no individual cabinetmaker could produce the large quantities demanded by American retail. A postwar survey of Danish design firms equipped to export furniture overseas reinforces the point.[19] The list was short, and cabinetmakers like Johannes Hansen were not on it.

In 1955 *Mobilia*, an international trade monthly about the Danish furniture industry, recommended that cabinetmakers resolve this limitation by organizing a manufacturing cooperative, with idle companies helping more active ones fill large orders.[20] This approach was used to fabricate Juhl's designs: Niels Vodder engaged subcontractors. To fabricate Juhl's Kaminstolen (or No. 45 chair, exhibited at and later bought by the Museum of Modern Art), he hired Ejnar Pedersen's shop, PP Møbler, which would make fifty at a time, then send them to Vodder to be stamped with his seal. In Pedersen's account, the Kaminstolen wasn't the only chair Vodder outsourced. Vodder's small workshop was often empty, and there was never more than one other cabinetmaker with him, "but there was lots of finished furniture."[21] Vodder made the Chieftain himself, but many other designs bearing his stamp were not made in his workshop.

Outsourcing to other workshops, Pedersen says, was good business, though it was also rather rare among cabinetmakers in the 1950s. Far more commonly, they collaborated with manufacturers—which also operated at a much smaller scale than was prevalent in the United States. As late as 1960, more than three-quarters of Danish furniture factories employed fewer than ten people (whereas cabinetmakers averaged closer to fifteen), and only a few were organized around thoroughly industrial production.[22] Manufacturing labor balanced handwork with industrial methods. What distinguished manufacturers from cabinetmakers was the former's eye toward sales and quantity production.

Many designers were already accustomed to working with manufacturers. (Wegner, for instance, had designed the line of modular office furnishings for Planmøbler and the bentwood Chinese chair for Fritz Han-

sen.) And as early as 1954, large-scale manufacturers like Fritz Hansen
or Søborg Møbelfabrik were invited to participate in the annual Cabinetmakers Exhibition on a rotating basis. This new alignment between cabinetmakers and manufacturers made it even easier for designers to move
between the two. While the interchange often entailed manufacturers
picking up designs conceived for cabinetmakers, it also went the other
way. For example, in 1959, cabinetmaker Willy Beck exhibited a chair
that Ejner Larsen and A. Bender Madsen had developed ten years earlier
for Fritz Hansen. Beck's version replaced the original beechwood with
oak, and refitted and sewed the leather seat and back. Juhl, too, used
his work for manufacturers to anchor new designs for cabinetmakers.
Simplified, geometric forms conceived in 1953 for a factory-produced
chair by France & Daverkosen (later France & Søn) reappeared in a 1961
bedroom suite for cabinetmaker Ludwig Pontoppidan.

In one contentious transaction, Niels Vodder outsourced fabrication
of Juhl's furniture to a factory where the designs could be made more
efficiently and priced accordingly.[23] Other cabinetmakers condemned
the arrangement as brazen and misleading, but this was only the most
extreme example of how industry and cabinetmakers were collaborating
more closely. No longer emphasizing the distinction, as they had when
their annual exhibition was launched in 1927, the cabinetmakers partnered with industry, understanding it as a crucial and necessary ally for
expanding into the American market.

Collaboration took various forms. Many manufacturers took designs
originally made by cabinetmakers and simplified them for easier, faster
construction. For example, when the manufacturer Bovirke began producing furniture by Juhl in the late 1940s, it made two chairs that were
pared-down versions of the No. 45 chair first made by Vodder. Except at

France & Søn, which grew its operation by mechanizing nearly every part of the production process, such variations and modifications were made less to accommodate machines (as would be the case with Juhl's idea to replace the Chieftain's step joint for Baker) than to scale up manual production. Later, Juhl would design new pieces for Bovirke with this specific goal in mind. In rarer cases, designs were conceived to accommodate a more thoroughly industrial production, with little handwork. For instance, in 1950, Wegner's former teacher O. Mølgaard-Nielsen and Peter Hvidt designed a line of furnishings for Fritz Hansen that could be made using a machine-driven lamination technique. Overall, the line between cabinetmaker and factory production was becoming increasingly blurry, particularly as cabinetmakers sought to scale up their output. In 1955, when a reporter asked Johannes Hansen about his most popular design (Wegner's Cow Horn chair from 1952), he replied good-humoredly, "Don't even ask about it. If I told you, my colleagues would claim that I am no longer a cabinetmaker."[24] Vodder, on the other hand, was less shy about his practices. When in September 1956 he published a thirty-page catalog with the Chieftain on its cover, the introduction proudly described his firm's "technical progress," "efficient working methods," and "serial production."[25]

Danish manufacturers also experimented with cooperative models to increase output. For example, in 1951 entrepreneur Ejvind Kold Christensen arranged a manufacturing partnership for the express purpose of distributing Wegner designs. The company, called SALESCO, involved five manufacturers, each responsible for a particular kind of furniture: Carl Hansen & Søn in Odense made chairs; Getama in West Jutland made upholstered furniture with wooden frames; A. P. Stolen in Copenhagen also made upholstered furniture (for which Ejnar Pedersen's PP Møbler would ultimately take on fabricating the wooden frames); Ry Møbler in central Jutland made storage furniture; and Andreas Tuck in Odense made tables. With tasks thus apportioned, the companies were collectively able to manufacture in quantity and distribute Wegner's designs abroad. A number of the designs SALESCO turned out were variations on pieces Wegner had first designed for Johannes Hansen.

The effort to serve the export market not only changed how designs were fabricated and, in some instances, required that they be modified. It also reshaped what materials were used, how items were shipped, and even considerations of taste. For example, while Hansen was creatively adapting the small-scale workshop model for large-scale production, Wegner was redesigning the Chair. The piece had debuted with an oak frame and its seat and back wrapped in cane—which concealed a conundrum. Unlike previous chairs he had designed, the Chair's back had no central, vertical support. The horizontal back rail thus required superior strength. Visually, the back and arms are continuous, a smoothly rotating strip, perpendicular to the ground across the back but parallel along the arms. Forming this structure from a single, solid piece of wood wouldn't work: the woodgrain—marking the wood's strongest axis—could run the length of the back *or* of the arms, but not both; and a cross-grain span for either would be susceptible to cracks. So arms and back were necessarily pieced together. For the Chair's debut, Wegner used dowels to attach the back to the arms and then, supposedly to hide the provisional construction, wrapped the back in cane to match the seat. Later he revised the design—and its construction—to incorporate the signature finger joint (fig. 2.2; see fig. 1.5). But still, the earliest version of the Chair continued to circulate. The version with the cane-wrapped back was selected for inclusion in the 1951 *Good Design* exhibition at MoMA, where its con-

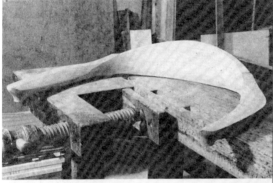

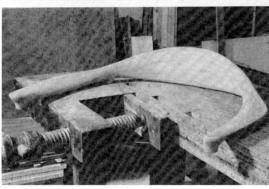

Figure 2.2
Process photographs
showing construction of
the Round Chair's top rail.
From Arne Karlsen and
Anker Tiedermann, *Made
in Denmark: A Picture-
Book about Modern
Danish Arts and Crafts*
(1960). Photograph:
Anker Tiedemann.

Figure 2.3 Edgar Kaufmann Jr. with Hans Wegner's Round Chair at the exhibition *Good Design*, Museum of Modern Art, New York, November 27, 1951–January 27, 1952. Gelatin silver print, 7½ × 9½ in. (19 × 24.1 cm). Photographic Archive, Museum of Modern Art Archives. Digital image © The Museum of Modern Art/licensed by SCALA/Art Resource, NY.

struction was attributed not to Johannes Hansen but to E. V. A. Nissen & Co., a Danish company specializing in rattan furniture (that may be an error on the part of the museum or an indication that Hansen's work-shop outsourced some of the labor on this run of the Chair; fig. 2.3).[26] In 1953 Hansen featured the version of the Chair with cane-wrapped seat and back in multiple displays at his newly opened storefront in Copenhagen's city center, and showed a version with a wood back and uphol-stered seat at the Cabinetmakers Exhibition (fig. 2.4a–b).[27] The American magazine *House Beautiful* featured the version with a cane-wrapped back on its cover, also in 1953, and included it again in June 1959 in a special issue titled "The Scandinavian Look in U.S. Homes" (plates 6 and 7).

The simultaneous circulation of three different versions of the Chair—with caned seat and back, with caned seat and unwrapped back, and with upholstered seat and unwrapped back—demonstrates that these were not stages in the design's evolution but variations on a theme designed to accommodate the demands of the market, and the export market in particular. For one, there was the matter of durability, which seems to have been of more concern to buyers than to magazine stylists. Just as the provisional doweled joints would have compromised the chair's strength over time, so too was caning an issue. "The cane breaks with wear or moisture," explained one American shopping guide, "and in our country reweaving is very expensive—if indeed you can find anyone to do it."[28] Removing the caning improved the chair's strength and ability to survive in a variety of climates, including humid American ones. This was important for Wegner's fabricator, Johannes Hansen, who, by the mid-1950s, was sending more than half of his workshop's production across the Atlantic.

As Danish design's geographic reach grew, cabinetmakers and man-ufacturers had to develop creative ways to manage the influx of orders and to fabricate furnishings suitable for disparate climates. After World War II, the mechanics of shipping also emerged as an industry concern. The Chair, for example, could be stacked, but crating it that way wasn't easy. Because associated costs contributed to a product's price abroad,

Figure 2.4a Display of Hans Wegner's furniture, including the Round Chair, in Johannes Hansen's store in central Copenhagen, 1953. *Møbler*, September 1953. Photographer unknown.

and thus its market viability, shipping was a matter of concern not just for export companies but among manufacturers and designers. (One American who ordered a Vodder-made Chieftain from Denmark in 1955 found the cost of shipping increased its price by close to 30 percent.[29]) France & Søn, a mattress company that in 1947 pivoted to furniture production, prioritized shipping as a primary element in the production process and adopted a flat-pack system that required package design to be part of the initial design phase for every new piece it put into production.[30] Some designers independently incorporated shipping considerations into their designs. For example, when Hvidt and Mølgaard-Nielsen designed the

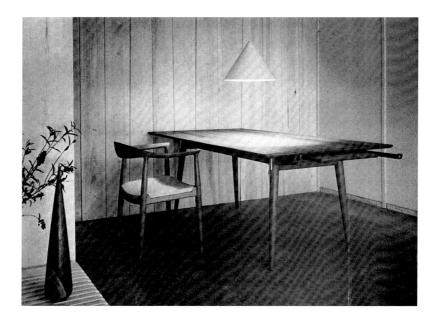

Figure 2.4b Johannes Hansen display featuring furniture, including the Round Chair, designed by Hans Wegner, Cabinetmakers Guild Exhibition, 1953. Photographer unknown.

Portex collection, its hallmark was that it could be shipped with ease. The sixteen pieces were designed to stack, fold, and knock down (fig. 2.5). Fourteen side tables could be piled, as flat packs, in a shipping crate that would hold only one assembled unit. A dining chair, folded, took up one-ninth the space of a standard chair.[31] The line employed wooden buttons in place of nails or screws, allowing consumers to complete the assembly without the use of tools. This emphasis on export extended even to the furniture's name: "Portex" is an inversion of *eksport*, the Danish word for export, with the *ks* replaced by an *x* to appear more international.[32] Ten years later, in 1955, Arne Hovmand-Olsen would take the concept even

Figure 2.5 Promotional images for Peter Hvidt and O. Mølgaard-Nielsen's Portex Collection, 1945. Landsforeningen Dansk Kunsthaandværk og Kunstindustri, Billedarkiv. DesignMuseum Danmark. Photographer unknown.

further, with a line of furnishings for Jutex (short for "Jutland Eksport," a cooperative of five small manufacturers, again replacing the Danish *ks* with a more international-looking *x*) that included six chairs, a sofa, a shelving unit, two tables, and a credenza with acrylic trays as shelves— all shipped together in a single compact crate. Unpacked and assembled, the upholstered seating and teak cabinetry cuffed in oak would furnish a small apartment. With brand names conceived for foreign markets and furniture designed for ease of shipping, these were, in the words of one Danish journalist, "models designed for export."[33]

Successful export also required the Danish furniture industry to become more sensitive to foreign, particularly American, tastes. The cultural attaché to the Danish consulate in New York told a Danish trade journal in 1951, "The young [American] family setting up home today places more importance on the acquisition of such goods as a TV set, a refrigerator, a washing machine and a car, than on articles which to the Danish way of thinking go to make up the furnishings of a home."[34] Fritz Hansen's managing director, Søren Hansen, echoed the assessment: "All Americans want are refrigerators, radios, and televisions."[35] To compete in this context, some Danes began designing furniture that acknowledged these priorities. Between 1953 and 1955, George Tanier, a New York–based importer of Scandinavian design, hired Juhl's former student Arne Vodder to develop a thirty-piece, modular furnishing system that included a range of combination television, radio, and record cabinets, and commissioned the small, family-run manufacturer Sibast Møbler, located fifty miles outside of Copenhagen, to fabricate the line. Much of its production was sent overseas. The rest was sold in Denmark, though there, too, it was likely marketed to Americans—in this case, tourists—as opposed to residents of Denmark, where televisions were still uncommon.

Foreign tastes began to reshape Danish furniture in other ways as well. Modern Danish designers had long been influenced by imported historic furniture: Wegner drew from a Qing Dynasty Chinese chair for his Round Chair; Kaare Klint riffed on a collapsible British Roorkhee chair for his Safari Chair (1933); cabinetmaker Frits Henningsen borrowed from a Shaker candlestand for an occasional table (1940); and beginning in the 1930s, textile designer Lis Ahlmann took inspiration from Japanese fabrics for her upholstery patterns. Danes also looked to contemporary furniture, an interest that was formally cultivated through initiatives like

American Design for Home and Decorative Use, an exhibition, curated by MoMA's Kaufmann and sponsored by the US government, that toured the Nordic countries in 1953, and the Lunning Prize, conceived by the director of the Georg Jensen store in New York and awarded annually to two Nordic designers, who were given money to study abroad. (When Wegner won in 1951, the prize's inaugural year, he used his award to travel to the United States.) Initiatives like these helped introduce Danish designers to contemporary American wares, which they had previously seen primarily in the pictures of trade magazines, and gave designers insight into American taste (or at least, in the case of the exhibition, what Kaufmann thought constituted "good" taste).[36] Increasingly in the 1950s, Danish designers incorporated American design style; for example, Arne Jacobsen took inspiration from the Eameses' plastic shells and Poul Kjærholm from Allan Gould's string chairs.[37] But they also incorporated popular preferences from overseas. When critics observed cabinetmakers upholstering their furniture in black leather, they concluded that "the explanation for this is that our furniture has primarily become an export product to the United States."[38]

Designers also adopted contemporary color palettes to dress up their designs for international appeal. In 1951, for instance, *Vogue*, already well circulated in Denmark and a reliable barometer of American fashion, ran a spread encouraging readers to combine pink and red garments and makeup ("the mix is newer than the match"; plate 8).[39] A few months later, Hvidt and Mølgaard-Nielsen featured a related color pairing in a mural, painted by Gunnar Aagaard Andersen, on the walls of their display at the Cabinetmakers Exhibition (plate 9). Though this color mix was not applied to the furniture itself, the subtle contrast on the wall played up the nuanced hues of its teak and cherry wooden elements and set off the complementary color of its upholstery, asserting the relevance of the furniture to contemporary American, and international, style. (As one reporter observed, it was a "super-American interior. . . . *House Beautiful* appears to have been the source of inspiration."[40]) In other instances, color was more directly incorporated into furnishings. In the summer of 1954, *Vogue*'s early report on fall fashion announced, "Blues . . . are important. Tangerine is the new young color."[41] And these were the very hues Juhl and others would soon use to upholster their furniture.

In the catalog accompanying a 1957 exhibition on the relation between textiles and furniture in Danish design, *arkitekt* Bent Salicath wrote that in the 1930s, textiles and furniture had mirrored one another in their "ascetic austerity." A new approach in textiles, led by weavers Gerda Henning and Marie Gudme Leth and aided by advances in textile printing, had occurred first; then designers began to realize "that the very simplicity of the furniture required a contrast in the richer utilization of colors."[42] Though Salicath explained the shift as motivated by formal concerns, the logic was also commercial. Color recipes were, by the 1950s, globally standardized, which allowed foreign buyers to match their Danish goods to other items in their homes, be they American-made or imported from elsewhere. As the *Shopping Guide to Europe* assured readers in its section on Denmark, buyers could, for a fee, take their "choice from [a] large stock of materials to get any effect desired."[43]

Offering such variety was yet another move Danish manufacturers made to cultivate American interest in Danish design, alongside attentiveness to the durability of materials and efficiency in shipping. In all of these ways, they altered or deliberately conceived designs not only to accommodate export but to facilitate it, while at the same time reorganizing production models to meet growing international demand.

Pricing for Americans

Even with Danish designers and manufacturers actively catering to the American market—designing for it and restructuring industry to scale up production—there remained obstacles to selling their wares in the United States. A 25 percent import duty on foreign goods meant that a chaise lounge retailing for $76 in Denmark would cost an American buyer $95, an already high price further inflated by shipping costs.[44] At the end of World War II, one Danish-born importer exploring what goods he could sell in the United States, realized that to compete on the American market, a chess set that cost him $53 to bring into the country could retail for no more than $35. "It is absolutely impossible," he concluded in a letter to Asger Fischer, director of the Danish design store Den Permanente.[45] Fourteen years later, a representative from Bonniers, a New York department store run by a Swedish publishing house, expressed similar concerns, also in a letter to Fischer, who was selecting objects for the American store to sell. "We have to have invoices and all the regular papers necessary for import," Fischer was told. "The duty will be about 25%, so you cannot choose museum pieces with fancy prices—it has to be commercially feasible."[46] The sale of Danish design abroad was as dependent upon trade agreements and tariffs as desirable styling and production capacities.

Beyond affecting what was produced and exported for sale overseas, tariffs influenced what materials Danish cabinetmakers and manufacturers used to fabricate their designs. As Wegner learned, certain materials, like caning, though widely available and inexpensive, were unsuitable for export to the United States. Others, like walnut, beech, and oak wood

Figure 2.6 Wood and veneer display, Cabinetmakers Guild Exhibition, undated. *Snedkerme-strene*, October 1960. Photographer unknown.

were available domestically but in limited quantities. (A mere 9 percent of Denmark—about fifteen hundred square miles—was forested, and people liked to say that Danish wood was used for fuel, not furniture.[47]) Most types of wood cabinetmakers used to fabricate furniture, including the six that were most popular in the early 1950s, were imported.[48] These foreign woods were so integral to the industry that after the war wood importers and distributors began participating in the annual Cabinetmakers Exhibitions. Before visitors even entered the building where the cabinetmakers' displays were set up, they walked through a courtyard full of logs, boards, veneers, and other samples (fig. 2.6).

Professional ties between the wood importers and the cabinetmakers were augmented by government interventions that bound their relationship in industry-shaping ways. In Denmark, Varedirektoratet (Ministry of Supply) was responsible for allocating imported materials and governing their prices through the application of tariffs, import taxes, and other added costs. Between 1945 and 1948, in speeches and in editorials, cabinetmakers implored the office to aid their industry, expressing dissatisfaction with high lumber prices that forced them either to use low-quality woods, rough with knots, or to charge more for their furniture.[49] Economic policy was, in this period, on the side of the cabinetmakers, prioritizing the import of raw materials for the production of exports, and once the Marshall Plan was instated, with a certain percentage of moneys earmarked for industrial development, the government was financially positioned to intervene.[50] With bureaucratic support and financial resources, the Ministry of Supply reversed the tariffs and taxes on wood and issued a subsidy in 1951. It put money into the industry and streamlined circulation by negotiating a deal to import teak, specifically, directly to the Danish distributors responsible for supplying the cabinetmakers with their wood.[51]

The Danish government subsidized teak not because cabinetmakers preferred it but because it was positioned to do so. Teak came from Thailand, where Denmark had maintained informal colonial ties since the nineteenth century, when, in an effort to avoid occupation by the French or the British, the Thai king made a deal with the Danish crown. While other European nations had acquired colonies, exploited their peoples, and turned their raw materials (rubber from the Belgian Congo, sugar from the British-ruled Barbados, and much, much more) into European wealth, Denmark's colonial holdings—including Greenland, the Faroe Islands, Tranquebar, a portion of the Gold Coast in present-day Ghana, and what are now known as the US Virgin Islands—were exploitative but never very profitable. Thailand was different. After signing a "treaty of friendship, commerce, and navigation" in May 1858, Danes were assigned strategic government positions and Danish industry and entrepreneurs received access to the country's minerals, tin, and teak, prized because it was perfect for building ships. The success of the Danish East Asiatic Company (EAC), for a time Scandinavia's most profitable company, was built on Thai teak. When Nils Anderson founded the company in 1897, its first route, from Bangkok to Copenhagen, was organized for the express purpose of sending teak to Denmark for the construction of more ships. Subsequent routes opened up new markets, advancing Denmark's capacity to import foreign goods and to export domestic products like furniture. Thai teak first facilitated the export of Danish furniture in the form of boats that could carry it, and later, when the government subsidy lowered the price of the wood, in the form of the furniture itself.

After the Ministry of Supply initiated the subsidy, teak took over. The same properties that made it suitable for the hull of a ship—it was durable and easy to bend—also made it an ideal material for the curve of a chair back. From 1952 to 1957 it was the most commonly used wood among Danish cabinetmakers and popular as well among manufacturers. (France & Søn, for example, used so much teak that it began having the wood cut to specifications in Thailand so that it would be easier to ship and faster to transform into furniture once it arrived in Denmark.[52]) As if to honor the wood's importance to the industry, when the Copenhagen department store Illums Bolighus, in 1959, put out a lavish two-hundred-page catalog highlighting Danish furniture, it was bound in teak veneer.

Teak's Thai origins were just as celebrated in Denmark as the material itself. At the 1954 Cabinetmakers Exhibition, held in a large Copenhagen convention center to commemorate the four hundredth anniversary of

Figure 2.7 Fritz Hansen display in front of wood display featuring photograph of logging, Cabinetmakers Guild Exhibition, 1954. Landsforeningen Dansk Kunsthaandværk og Kunstindustri, Billedarkiv. DesignMuseum Danmark. Photographer unknown.

Figure 2.8 (*facing page*) King Bhumibol Adulyadej of Thailand, Søren Christian Hansen, King Frederick IX of Denmark, and Poul Fritz Hansen at the Fritz Hansen factory, 1960. *Danish Foreign Office Journal* (1960). Photographer unknown.

the Cabinetmakers Guild, an enormous photograph, two stories tall, of Thai loggers dressed one wall of the exhibition space (fig. 2.7). In 1960, when Denmark welcomed King Bhumibol Adulyadej of Thailand, the Danish press made much of his visits to furniture factories. "Søren and Fritz Hansen are showing the kings how Thai teak becomes Danish furniture," read the caption accompanying a photograph from his and Danish king Frederick IX's trip to the Fritz Hansen factory (fig. 2.8).[53] Within the

Danish furniture industry, the foreign origin of its raw materials was well publicized and celebrated as an example of successful globalism. But, amid decolonization efforts around the globe, the Thai government was rethinking the terms of its relationship with Denmark.

By the time King Bhumibol visited Copenhagen, teak was in decline among the cabinetmakers. Danish papers offered eulogies, observing that rosewood had replaced it as the industry's preferred wood. While most reports attributed this to changing tastes, two let slip a different story.[54] One article explained that the international fad for teak furniture, sparked by Denmark, had driven demand so high as to result in short-ages.[55] The other explained that rosewood, though expensive, could be sliced extremely thin for veneers and so made affordable.[56] Both were true but did little to explain the real cause of the shift. In fact, teak's fall from favor owed to Thailand's efforts to renegotiate its agreement with Denmark, part of a larger bid for economic independence and local control of native resources. Under the new agreement, the Ministry of Supply could no longer control the price of Thai teak. Calls for conser-vation further restricted Danish teak farming in Thailand. Teak became less popular within the Danish furniture industry because Thailand now controlled how and where it was grown and exported. Between 1960 and 1961, teak exports to Denmark declined by more than 50 percent.[57]

The decline of teak threatened not only the industry's narrative of growth and overseas success but the international identity of Danish design. By aiding the furniture industry with a teak subsidy, the Dan-ish government had inadvertently helped brand the country's furniture, making it recognizable to American consumers by way of its material—the *Washington Post* would herald the postwar period as "the era of Danish *teak* furniture."[58] When in 1958 a selection of Danish furniture premiered in Chicago at a popular State Street store, a *Chicago Tri-bune* journalist lauded the wood's pervasiveness: "Even the drawer pulls are teak." But she was most impressed by the fact that this was Danish furniture designed for Americans. "The grouping is exceptional," she wrote. "It was designed and made in Denmark especially for the United States market, with the help of American merchandisers so that more than ever it fits the American home and way of life."[59] Even in America, it was no secret that Denmark's teak furniture was designed and made specifically for the United States. With the support of the government, Danish designers and furniture makers had redesigned their objects and approaches as a way to popularize Danish design abroad, reinventing it in the process.

: : :

Shortly after he began collaborating with Baker, Finn Juhl received an invitation from Nordenfjeldske Kunstindustrimuseum (National Museum of Decorative Arts) in Trondheim, Norway, to design *Interior-52*, a period room exemplifying Danish design at midcentury (plate 10). The room was to be installed alongside a mid-nineteenth-century room modeled after one designed by William Morris and a turn-of-the-twentieth-century interior filled with furniture by Henry van de Velde. Breaking with the brief, which specified Danish design, Juhl included birch plywood stools designed (by Alvar Aalto) and manufactured (by Artek) in Finland and a chair designed (by Charles and Ray Eames) and manufactured (by Herman Miller) in the United States. But as in the museum's other period rooms, each of which highlighted the work of a single designer, most of the furniture was Juhl's own. Some of the pieces were made in Denmark by Niels Vodder, others (the desk and desk chair) in the United

States by Baker. And the American company paid for the installation's Chieftain, though it was Vodder who made it.[60] Before *Interior-52* was unveiled in Norway, Juhl planned to preview it, minus the Aalto stools and the Eames chair, in Denmark at the 1952 Cabinetmakers Exhibition. But organizers refused to allow him to exhibit the Baker-made goods; only cabinetmaker-made furniture was allowed. So Vodder reproduced (or contracted out) the desk and the chair specifically for display in Denmark. Even so, American influence made its way into the exhibition, concealed in the form of the Vodder-made, but Baker-funded, Chieftain.

This anecdote is emblematic of the Danish furniture industry in the 1950s, when production models and designs were reconfigured to serve an American market, and government intervention in the form of the teak subsidy made it economically possible for the industry to compete in that market. If the cabinetmakers' demand that Vodder remake the Baker-manufactured Juhl designs suggests an unwillingness to acknowledge the extent to which the United States was already infiltrating Danish design, the Danish government was more matter-of-fact about it. When the Danish minister of culture accepted an invitation for the country to participate in the 1951 Milan Triennale, an international design exhibition and competition colloquially known as a design Olympics, Denmark—whose exhibition committee included representatives from the Foreign Office and the Ministry of Commerce alongside designers and museum personnel—proudly exhibited Danish-made goods alongside Juhl-designed furniture made by Baker in America.[61] In both its display and its organizational makeup, Denmark's representation at the Triennale acknowledged an underlying truth: Danish design was an international affair.

3

At Home
with Danish Design

On Easter Sunday 1954, a twenty-nine-year-old American woman named Doris Scherbak wrote to Asger Fischer, director of the Copenhagen store Den Permanente, to inquire about ordering a pair of Round Chairs. So that there would be no confusion about the design or version she had in mind, she included a picture of the Chair torn from a magazine (fig. 3.1). Scherbak was living in Paris, where her husband Boris—Bob, as she called him—had been stationed. Bob worked on the Marshall Plan, and the Scherbaks were preparing to move into newly built, government-sponsored housing in Neuilly, an embassy-rich area adjacent to the French capital. "The flats are modern, well-planned, efficient, light and airy with large terraces," Scherbak wrote, as though transcribing from a brochure. They had "practical kitchens and bathrooms, really most American-looking." The apartments, she explained, came with a Wegner chair and "modern, good-looking furniture" by the American manufacturer Knoll Associates.[1] The Scherbaks finished outfitting their home with Danish ceramics, furniture, and fabrics from Den Permanente, including a wooden toy elephant Fischer had sent as a gift. (Scherbak's husband and son named it Herman. "He is now one of the family," she wrote in her thank you note.[2]) They expected that their Danish purchases would be well suited to their new, American-style home. "We are anticipating being able to display our beautiful Danish things in appropriate surroundings for the first time since we got them," Scherbak concluded. "I think it's going to be an apartment to be proud of."[3]

The letter, filed among Fischer's correspondence, is a telling archival document in that it triangulates the three major players responsible for the popular rise of Danish furniture among Americans. First, there is Scherbak, an American consumer interested in buying Danish design. Then, evident in the torn magazine page, are the tastemakers who chose to feature Wegner's Chair and wrote the caption communicating its achievement ("almost wholly transparent" with a "sculptured frame"). Finally, there is Fischer, who sold not only furniture, ceramics, textiles, and other designed objects but also, alongside exhibition designers, filmmakers, and others, Danish design as an idea.

On their face, these positions seem distinct. Sellers had a vested interest—economic, nationalist, or otherwise—in promoting and distributing the furniture. Consumers, with their spending, affirmed its popularity and contributed to the Danish industry's growth. And tastemakers were professionals who, through formal publication or presentation outlets (lecture halls, magazines, museums), told "nonprofessionals what their taste should be," as cultural critic Russell Lynes wrote in *The Tastemakers*, published in 1954, when the Danish design craze was gaining momentum. In practice, however, roles were often blurred. Sellers and tastemakers were both involved in organizing exhibitions featuring Danish design, often yoking it to Scandinavian design more generally.

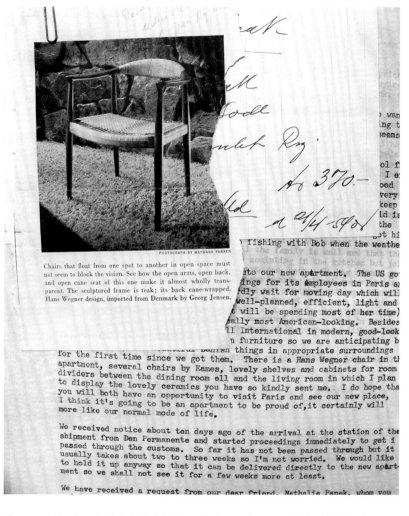

PHOTOGRAPH BY MAYNARD PARKER

Chairs that float from one spot to another in open space must not seem to block the vision. See how the open arms, open back, and open cane seat of this one make it almost wholly transparent. The sculptured frame is teak; its back cane-wrapped. Hans Wegner design, imported from Denmark by Georg Jensen.

...to our new apartment. The US go ...ings for its employees in Paris a ...dly wait for moving day which wil ...well-planned, efficient, light and ...t will be spending most of her time) ...ally most American-looking. Besides ...ll International in modern, good-look ...n furniture so we are anticipating b ...things in appropriate surroundings for the first time since we got them. There is a Hans Wegner chair in th apartment, several chairs by Eames, lovely shelves and cabinets for room dividers between the dining room ell and the living room in which I plan to display the lovely ceramics you have so kindly sent me. I do hope tha you will both have an opportunity to visit Paris and see our new place, I think it's going to be an apartment to be proud of, it certainly will more like our normal mode of life.

We received notice about ten days ago of the arrival at the station of the shipment from Den Permanente and started proceedings immediately to get i passed through the customs. So far it has not been passed through but it usually takes about two to three weeks so I'm not worried. We would like to hold it up anyway so that it can be delivered directly to the new apart- ment so we shall not see it for a few weeks more at least.

We have received a request from our dear friend, Nathalie Panek, whom you

Figure 3.1 Letter from Doris Scherbak to Asger Fischer, April 1954, enclosing clipping about Hans Wegner's Round Chair. Photograph by the author.

Tastemakers were also consumers. MoMA curator Edgar Kaufmann Jr., for example, bought a Juhl No. 45 chair for his personal use. (It's now on display in Fallingwater, the Frank Lloyd Wright–designed house commissioned by Kaufmann's father, which Kaufmann entrusted to the Western Pennsylvania Conservancy for protection and preservation in the early 1960s.) And consumers were ad hoc tastemakers, not just buying furniture but showing it off in their homes and offices, sharing their appreciation for Danish design within their social and professional circles.

Scherbak offers a prime example of how consumers—while not delivering lectures, organizing exhibitions, or publishing articles in magazines—still had a hand in disseminating design. Friends in Paris, she writes in her letter to Fischer, "are interested in buying a pair of these chairs with the cane seat, but with no cane on the back, simply the wood frame, in teak as shown. Is this possible and how much?"[4] Not limiting her role to shopping, she acts as an intermediary, helping her friends get the chairs they want, facilitating the furniture's spread through informal channels. Scherbak was just one of many for whom the purchase of Danish design was as much a social affair as a retail experience. Her letter, ostensibly inquiring about the Chair, is full of life updates about the upcoming move and Bob's new hobbies ("sculpting and modeling"). Over the years, she wrote many letters to Fischer. Friendships like theirs—the Scherbaks would later travel with Fischer and his wife on holiday to Mexico—and social networks more generally, contributed, alongside professional exchanges, to the furniture's rise. Together with sellers and tastemakers, consumers transformed Danish design into an international phenomenon.

Sellers

Scherbak knew to write to Fischer about the Round Chairs because she had previously shopped at his store, buying, among other things, a record player, nesting tables, and a loveseat. In the 1950s, Fischer's store, Den Permanente, was Denmark's go-to spot for Danish design. There, Juhl's Chieftain, which graced the showroom floor into the mid-1960s, and Wegner's Chair were displayed and sold alongside other cabinetmaker-made furniture carefully selected by a jury who claimed to be less concerned with salability than with the quality of the goods. (The store's full name, Den Permanente udstilling af dansk kunsthaand-værk og kunstindustri—The Permanent Exhibit of Danish Handcraft and Industrial Design—gestured at this priority.) In addition to furniture, there was silver, porcelain, jewelry, glassware, lighting, textiles, toys, and art, all designed and made in Denmark. Housed in Vesterport, a glass-fronted, two-story building directly across from Copenhagen's central train station, the twenty-thousand-square-foot store presented tourists freshly arrived in the nation's capital with a carefully curated picture of Danish design.

Scherbak's inquiry surely pleased Fischer, who was hard at work increasing the international audience for Danish design. From its founding in 1931, Den Permanente had welcomed foreigners, offering, among other services, salespeople fluent in French, German, and English. Already in 1934, it had established a committee for "Tourist Propa-ganda," whose work concentrated on enticing buyers from abroad. And the store had a hand in organizing the two-year traveling retail exhi-bition of Danish design that followed the 1939 New York World's Fair.

Fischer was particularly enthusiastic about cultivating American buyers. Almost immediately after he was appointed managing director in 1945, he toured the United States. To stay current on American sales strategies, he subscribed to *Merchants Record and Show Window*, an American trade journal about display, and collected mail-order catalogs from companies like Sears.[5] He conceived of a new department dedicated to "tourist arts," a delicate term for souvenir items like hand-sewn dolls and painted plates, and in 1950 established an export bureau offering shipping services, which helped foreign buyers, particularly Americans navigating the complex web of rules and restrictions that characterized US customs. (Returning residents were allowed a duty-free exemption on purchases up to $500 if they had been out of the US more than twelve days, but only $200 for travels of more than two but less than twelve days—and in either case, only if they had not claimed the exemption in the preceding thirty-one days. Purchases above $500 were dutiable, but buyers could strategize to apply the exemption to the goods taxed at the highest rate. And so on . . .[6]) Den Permanente also began offering shared shipment options; if Scherbak's friends did order a pair of Chairs, they could choose to have them packed with other goods headed to Paris, and thus pay less. Fischer placed ads for the store in tourism brochures, specifically targeting those in English. Den Permanente was where "You ought to buy your souvenirs," declared one postwar ad that appeared in English-language leaflets.[7]

Beyond pursuing consumers with enticing displays, service conveniences, and strategic marketing, Fischer also courted American tastemakers. When *Interiors* first published pictures of the Chieftain and the Chair, the magazine was inundated with queries about the two designs. But getting them into the magazine to begin with required behind-the-scenes machinations. Fischer was one of many participants in the Danish furniture industry—and the Nordic design field more broadly—who promoted national design overseas by cultivating relationships with American design professionals. (Juhl, for instance, established what would become a long-standing friendship with Edgar Kaufmann Jr. after Kaufmann toured Denmark in 1948.) But in his role as director of a retail establishment that sold a carefully curated selection of Danish things, Fischer was especially well positioned and particularly influential. He hosted luncheons for home economics editors from newspapers like Cleveland's *Plain Dealer* and the *Los Angeles Times*, staged his shop for photo spreads in magazines like *House and Garden*, and arranged tours of Den Permanente for members of the US Embassy, its staff, and their families.[8] In other contexts, too, he served as an ambassador for Danish design, writing for publications circulated by American furniture associations, exchanging exhibition catalogs with the director of design at Corning Glass Works, and lecturing on Danish craft at the first annual Conference of American Craftsmen.[9] Given the vast array of goods sold in his store, Fischer was the perfect attaché. He could talk about furniture alongside ceramics, toys alongside jewelry.

Fischer brought together disparate objects to tell a common story of Danish design as founded in "quality and craftsmanship," characteristics Den Permanente had highlighted from the start.[10] "The human touch always will be in what they are doing," he wrote of Danish designers in a statement for the National Retail Furniture Association in 1958.[11] Though it was true that the store showcased the work of craftsmen rather than manufacturers, whose products were not considered by its jury, praising human touch was part of a broader marketing strategy invented to promote a specific idea of Danish design as a craft-based, heritage culture.

At Den Permanente and also beyond it, the Chieftain, the Chair, and other Danish design were sold using this story.

Fischer was one of many, before and after the war, who anchored their marketing of Danish design in craftsmanship. In 1939 the Danish pavilion at the New York World's Fair had taken just this approach. Prepared by Den Permanente and the Danish Society of Arts and Crafts (in 1954, industrial design was added to its mission), the catalog lauded the "genuine, professional workmanship" of "several notable handicraftsmen" and explained that the country's "best works are characterized by the will to produce genuine, technical workmanship."[12] (To ensure that this craftsmanship wasn't mistaken for backwardness, the catalog also noted a predilection for "investigation and solution in accordance with the exigencies of the times."[13]) The prominence of craft was often reiterated, particularly in industry- and government-sanctioned materials. In 1947, for example, a short, government-sponsored film produced for foreign markets focused on Danish applied arts and highlighted craftsmanship. During the next decade and a half, *Shaped by Danish Hands* was shown across the English-speaking world, including at a National Research Council program in Ottawa, Canada (1949), a women's film night at a YMCA in Canberra, Australia (1954), and a Beta Sigma Phi meeting in Columbia, Washington (1964).[14] The film introduced audiences to Danish ceramics, furniture, and silver, connecting them through a shared emphasis on craft. Recurring close-up shots of makers' hands made the point visually. The voice-over reinforced it. "In the soil of Denmark," explained the narrator, "pieces of earthenware vessels shaped by unknown forefathers scores of generations back can still be found." Commitment to craft, the film suggests, unifies postwar design in Denmark across media and over time, and is embedded in its very territory.[15] This link between Danish craftsmanship and Danish land was more than incidental; it was actively cultivated through an emphasis on the natural—natural materials, natural resources, and natural inclinations.

The film was made before either the Chieftain or the Chair had been conceived, but a brief segment on Juhl quotes the *arkitekt*: "Furniture should be so made that you get the urge to feel the wood . . . that warm and living character that causes one's fingers to tingle."[16] The importance of the hand, he proposes, is not limited to the maker's skill but extends to the experience of the user. In Juhl's telling, this link is forged through the furniture's characteristic material: wood. Juhl's belief in wood's unique status as a living material was shared by many of his *arkitekt* and cabinetmaker colleagues and by others, as designer Børge Jensen observed, beyond the sphere of professionals. "It is quite usual," Jensen writes, "for people to say that wood 'shrinks' or 'expands', that it 'cracks' or 'splits', and that it 'twists', 'warps' or 'buckles', and it is actually a fact that wood can conduct itself just as these expressions indicate."[17] For Jensen, this was evidence that wood, "no matter how old it may be after felling and final preparation," always remains alive, even in the living room. Along with the narrative of craftsmanship, sellers and industry professionals presented the furniture's living quality as a mark of distinction that elevated Danish design in an era of synthetic materials and mass manufacture.

This approach to marketing built on connections between design and nature that other Nordic countries had already begun to forge in the United States and elsewhere. In these narratives, too, wood was central. Alvar Aalto's design for the Finnish pavilion at the 1939 New York World's Fair had celebrated wood as foundational to his nation's economic and social health. Large photographs suspended on an undulating wall composed of vertical wooden slats pictured Finnish wood transformed into exports like paper, skis, and furniture, with samples of these items, arranged in patterns, displayed beneath. Similarly, the fair's Swedish exhibition was designed, in the words of the accompanying brochure, to highlight the country's "most important natural resources." A central garden was landscaped with white birch trees, "so typical of Sweden." Inside, photographs of the Swedish countryside greeted visitors, and evergreen logs displayed like columns, extending the full height of the building, highlighted the forest products that at the time constituted half of Sweden's exports.[18] While these displays presented wood, in particular, as formative for Finland's and Sweden's industries, and thus their economies, postwar narratives emphasized it as fundamental to national character.

An image of nature unfettered by industry often figured in presentations of Danish design for foreign audiences. At Den Permanente, large plants and fresh flowers accompanied furniture displays, gesturing at the connection between national design and national land. The concept was advanced more officially in *Design in Scandinavia*, an exhibition of more than seven hundred objects curated and designed by representatives from Denmark, Finland, Norway, and Sweden that toured twenty-three North American cities between 1953 and 1957.[19] Its opening gallery introduced each participating country with an image of an object produced there alongside an oversize photograph of its landscape (fig. 3.2). Planters with tropical philodendrons and trellised vines were placed around the gallery. Though the selection of plants was more at home in the midcentury modern interiors staged for magazine spreads than the Nordic wilderness, it had the effect of emphasizing the importance of nature to the designed objects on display, which included the Chieftain

Figure 3.2 *Design in Scandinavia*, installation view, San Francisco Museum of Art, 1957. Rijksarkivet, Oslo. Image courtesy of Jørn Guldberg.

and the Chair. Building upon a concept of regional design developed over the past hundred years, the exhibition catalog noted the prevalence of "artisan production" and "the handmade product" throughout the Nordic countries, inflected by the presence of "national features that are given expression in [each country's] creative art . . . due to geographical differences."[20] While craftsmanship united design across the region, nature—Norway's mountains and fjords, Finland's lakes and forests, Sweden's birch coppices—introduced differences that shaped distinct national design traditions. Danish design was presented as inextricable from Denmark's "green fields, trim farms, and rolling heath."[21] Whereas prewar exhibitions in Sweden and Finland had presented nature as raw material to fuel industry, thus signifying national strength, here nature helped establish unique national design identities for distinct countries that, for economic reasons, sought to brand themselves collectively as Scandinavian. Programs accompanying the exhibition, including public lecture series and radio and television features highlighting Scandinavian music and literature, reiterated the point, and Juhl advanced it further when he told a writer for *Look* magazine that "Danish designers are influenced by the Danish landscape." He drew particular attention to the terrain's "soft curves," which are also evident in, among other places, the enveloping form of the Chieftain and the rounded back of the Chair.[22] Rather than attaching Danish design to its formative institutions—the Royal Academy School of Architecture, the Cabinetmaker Day School, the Cabinetmakers Exhibitions—Juhl and other purveyors of Danish design insisted on its character as naturally given. This was a marketing narrative designed for export, a way of insisting upon the essential Danishness of Danish design.

Ironically, *Design in Scandinavia* put the fact of this fiction on veiled display. In the first gallery, where the other nations showed only a pair of images, Denmark also exhibited an object. Alongside an enlarged photograph of farmland dusted with woods and a drawing of Peter Hvidt and O. Mølgaard-Nielsen's AX chair, the chair itself sat on a plinth. (In the United States, the chair was sold as the FH chair or Hansen chair.) It was a curious choice to illustrate the connection between the nation's territory and homegrown craftsmanship. Not only had the AX chair been made in a factory by the manufacturer Fritz Hansen, and from a combination of Danish beech and imported teak, it had, like the narrative that accompanied it, been conceived specifically for export.

The AX chair's inclusion in the introductory gallery is also compelling in that it insists upon a modern version of craftsmanship that extends beyond the workshop. Either the Chieftain or the Chair would have introduced a more straightforward story of a craft tradition in which workshop artisans turn out pieces by hand. (This is particularly apparent when comparing iterations of the Chieftain, whose details, including the horned cap on either side of the seat back, the tabs beneath the seat to keep it in place, and the vertical stiles on either side of the chair back, varied in structure, material, and placement, evidence of a flexible workshop practice open to experimentation and contingent upon material availability and efficiency.[23] Of course, a single instance of the design cannot communicate this.) The AX, by contrast, was made in a factory, presenting a vision of craftsmanship updated for the twentieth century.

This idea was reiterated in promotional materials designed to sell Danish design to foreign audiences. Take the 1960 book *Made in Denmark: A Picture-Book about Modern Danish Arts and Crafts*, a veritable ode to Danish handicraft, published in Denmark for English-language readers. One section, "The Cabinetmaker," focuses on the production of Wegner's Chair, illustrated with close-up photographs of a fabricator's hands working wood (fig. 3.3a). Another section, "The Factory," also shows hands, here working in tandem with machines, emphasizing the crafted nature of the factory-made object (fig. 3.3b). Manual skill, the photos suggest, was not just the hallmark of workshop craftsmen; it was also required in the Danish factories that turned out furniture. "Even in the large industrial establishments a great part of the working process is carried out by hand," confirmed *arkitekt* Esbjørn Hiort, one of Juhl's

Figure 3.3a
Cabinetmaker constructing the Round Chair. From Arne Karlsen and Anker Tiedermann, *Made in Denmark: A Picture-Book about Modern Danish Arts and Crafts* (1960). Photograph: Anker Tiedemann.

Figure 3.3b
Factory worker manually operating a machine transforming veneer layers into a chair shell. From Arne Karlsen and Anker Tiedermann, *Made in Denmark: A Picture-Book about Modern Danish Arts and Crafts* (1960). Photograph: Anker Tiedemann.

Figure 3.4 Cabinetmaker constructing the Round Chair. From B. D., "Hans Wegner: The Heresies of a Quiet Dane," *Industrial Design*, March 1959. Photographer unknown.

classmates at the Royal Academy, in the catalog accompanying *The Arts of Denmark: Viking to Modern*, an exhibition that opened at the Metropolitan Museum of Art in New York in 1960 and was widely publicized by the Danish government.[24] Skilled handwork was a fact of the Danish industry, but craftsmanship was part of a story sold to Americans alongside the furniture.

Americans bought it. "Careful craftsmanship, fine finishes and a neat light line . . . are characteristic," wrote Betty Pepis in the *New York Times* in 1950.[25] John Stuart Inc. called the high-end, factory-made furniture it imported from Denmark "The Danish Craftsmen Series." And when the trade magazine *Industrial Design* published an article on Wegner, the author commended "his sensitive and poetic handling of wood," as though the craftsman was the designer and not the cabinetmaker whose unattributed likeness, shown at work, was used to illustrate the article (fig. 3.4).[26] These associations were framed as inherently Danish. "Denmark is a country of exuberance," wrote Marilyn Hoffman in the *Christian Science Monitor*, repeating the narrative of national design as a natural given, "a land where fantasy and imagination reach out and touch everything and are the chief ingredients of Danish design."[27] As tastemakers in the United States picked up on this trope of craftsmanship, they would also recast it as a marker of American values.

Tastemakers

In the mid-1950s, Edgar Kaufmann Jr. delivered a lecture at Columbia University celebrating the work of Finn Juhl. Though he did not mention specific furniture pieces, his reference to the way Juhl's chairs "seem to rule their environments" suggests he had in mind the regal Chieftain.[28] Kaufmann began by comparing the supposedly Danish approach to the machine—described as a tool for harnessing creativity—to that of Frank Lloyd Wright, at the time America's most celebrated architect. And he concluded with the declaration that "we would feel less American, without Finn Juhl's work around us."[29] Framing Juhl's contribution in terms of American achievement and affect, Kaufmann was one of many midcentury American tastemakers who lauded Danish design (or, more commonly, Scandinavian design) for what it meant to their own culture.

Some grounded the resonance of Danish design in resemblance. When the Chieftain and the Chair made their American debut in the pages of *Interiors*, the accompanying descriptions identified them as objects of nature, the Chieftain a plant with "each section like a living branch," the Chair a body, its "sturdy legs . . . muscular rather than overfed."[30] No reference was made to the objects that had accompanied the Chieftain in its Danish showing—the archer's bow, the photograph of an African hunter. Instead, similes of living branches and muscular legs invoked both the idea of the natural promoted by Danish sellers and an idea of "organic design" already prevalent in a certain strand of postwar American design.

Deployed in the early 1940s, less to describe furnishings that looked like flora or fauna than furnishings that behaved like them, "organic design" referred to objects that were harmoniously structured and shaped to best serve their intended purpose.[31] This definition, which freed the organic from the yoke of natural materials or natural forms, allowed the term to be applied to the vital, shapely forms of industrially produced furniture by designers like Charles Eames, Eero Saarinen, the Danish-born émigré Jens Risom, and others frequently featured on the pages of *Interiors*. By using the language of the living to describe the Chieftain, the Chair, and other items from the 1949 Cabinetmakers Exhibition, the magazine subtly evoked a likeness between contemporary American design and its Danish counterpart. Affirming the similarity more explicitly, *Interiors* noted, of Danish chairs in particular, that "the designers have translated the bulkless look of modern buildings into an attempt to minimize the strength it takes to support a relaxed human being (an attempt that in this country [the United States] is sold as a space-saving device)." In other words, the magazine observed a shared tendency in Danish and American design toward compact, pared-down forms. The Chieftain, the Chair, and other furniture pieces from the 1949 exhibition were commended for their concord with American design trends.

A decade later, in his contribution to the *Arts of Denmark* exhibition catalog, Kaufmann reiterated the point. He compared Georg Jensen to Tiffany, Danish silver and Royal Copenhagen porcelain to American jazz and Fiberglass, and the partnerships between cabinetmakers and *arkitekts* to those forged by American companies and industrial designers in the 1930s.[32] Americans and Danes, he insisted, are both drawn to "organic design . . . [which] blends form, structure and utility into a vivid whole." This, he explained, "is why Americans, like so many others, feel firmly drawn to even daring examples of Danish design."[33] According to Kaufmann, Denmark's design culture twinned America's.

Others saw in this likeness a causal relationship. Landscape architect Christopher Tunnard and architecture critic Henry Hope Reed went so far as to locate the foundational kernel of inspiration behind postwar Danish design in American Shaker furniture.[34] They were right to discern a Shaker influence, brought to Denmark through objects and, even more so, Depression-era publications by Faith and Edward Deming Andrews, but it was just one of many imported references, which also included nineteenth-century British safari chairs, ancient Egyptian folding stools, and the Chinese Qing Dynasty chairs that inspired Wegner's Round Chair.[35] Tunnard and Reed overstated their claim because they, like Kaufmann, who presented America's cultural production as a barometer for evaluating the success of Denmark's, used Danish design to laud American creativity.

Others used Danish design, and Scandinavian design more generally, as an opportunity to resuscitate and refine popular American style. When *Design in Scandinavia* opened in 1954, Leslie Cheek Jr., the exhibition's American coordinator and director of the Virginia Museum of Fine Arts, where it premiered, wrote about how Scandinavian design could serve America as a model. He lauded it as "a spiritual expression" of the region's people. Regional design, he suggested, telegraphed regional tastes. Homing in on the narrative of craftsmanship put forward in the exhibit, he insisted, "Even the poorest [in Denmark] is aware of the virtues of the hand-made article." He contrasted this to American taste, which he described as "derivative, unsure of itself," and "relatively low," but assured readers that Scandinavian design could foster a revival of craft in America that would reshape mass production and improve popular taste. "The sturdy and honorable and beautiful pieces from Scandinavia," he wrote, "will provide some impetus for a greater, more human utilization of the truly remarkable means at our disposal in America."[36] Scandinavian design mattered, Cheek suggested, because it provided a template the United States could use to reimagine its own future.

Cheek's observations differed from Kaufmann's not only insofar as they presented Nordic design culture as a model for improvement rather than a mirror of analogous successes, but also in that Cheek considered Scandinavian design culture generally, while Kaufmann had focused on Denmark. This regional view was common among American tastemakers, who were often responding to collective export initiatives like the *Design in Scandinavia* exhibition. Before the war, at a 1937 meeting of Nordic delegates to discuss economic cooperation, Danish representatives had proposed a "permanent collaboration . . . by the respective countries in international exhibitions,"[37] but it was not until the 1950s that the proposal was realized, due largely to financial necessity. For example, when a number of Swedish industries were unable to pay the exhibition fees required to participate in the 1951 Milan Triennale, an important international design competition, the Swedish organizing committee invited Denmark, Finland, and Norway to share the country's pavilion. (Norway, which had not received an invitation from the Triennale's organizing committee, declined.) While this exhibition connected design from several Nordic countries as a matter of regional proximity, other international exhibitions solidified the connection through the concept of Scandinavian design, developed by Scandinavians with an eye to foreign markets and popularized by foreign design professionals like Cheek who helped shape those markets.

In the catalog accompanying *Design in Scandinavia*, Swedish critic Gotthard Johansson wrote, "Scandinavian design to-day is created for the people of to-day, people who live under conditions which are essentially much the same as those of the average American."[38] *House Beautiful* editor Elizabeth Gordon, who had a hand in initiating *Design in Scandinavia*, repeated the idea in an article published in February 1954, a month after the exhibition opened, but inflected it with additional implication. While Johansson suggested that Scandinavian design was

relevant to both Nordic and American citizens because of similar circumstances he left unspecified, Gordon spelled out the connection: "Why
are the home furnishings so well designed and so full of meaning for us?"
she asked. "Because they are so well designed and so full of meaning for
the Scandinavians themselves. Aimed at Scandinavian home life, their
designs have a natural beauty and usefulness for our own, for we are
both deeply democratic people."[39] For Gordon, Scandinavian culture
aligned with American democracy. In the context of the Cold War, the
comparison animated the importance of design and domestic life for
America's political future.

Gordon's explicit politicization of the likeness between Scandinavians and Americans recalled similar claims made during the interwar
period, when the United States was embroiled in debates about immi-
gration. Then, as the popular press reported the comfortable assimilation of Scandinavian immigrants to the US, for whom "the traditions
of the homeland" did not "clash with their new citizenship," outspoken
eugenicists like Madison Grant advocated increasing the number of visas
offered to those from Nordic countries so as to reinforce "the blood
that made America what it is."[40] The logic of eugenics made its way into
1930s American design that imagined a future of improved dwellings and
perfected people to inhabit them, and the specific connection between
Nordic peoples and what Grant called "native" Americans (by which he
meant colonizing settlers) would remain a foundational myth. Decades
later, in a reflection on the popularity of wooden furniture in the United
States, the British architecture critic Reyner Banham would describe
wood as "the material of the northern forests where most [Americans]
come from, the original environment of our human stock and many of
our most valued social concepts, such as practical equality and democ-

racy."[41] Gordon's postwar claims about the connection between Scandinavian and American culture did not explicitly state such a faulty (and racist) assertion about "original" (and, by implication, authentic) American culture. But, consciously or not, her assumption of a shared essential identity demonstrates the idea's nefarious pervasiveness, which she invoked in the service of an argument about design's role in the Cold War contest.

Five years later, in a special issue of *House Beautiful*, Gordon would reanimate this argument, describing Scandinavian design as "very democratic" and "a people's art," possessed of "universal" beauty and "able to speak to all."[42] For Gordon, Scandinavian design offered a much-needed counterpoint to the "gibberish of Modernism"—think Ludwig Mies van der Rohe, Le Corbusier, and Marcel Breuer—which "only the initiated few were able to grasp."[43] This was not the first time Gordon had condemned Miesian modernism. Previously, in an article that termed modernism a national threat, she had described the movement's leading proponents as "would-be 'Artistic Dictators'" aiming to invade "the heart of our society—the home," and thus American society itself.[44] By contrast, the Chieftain, the Chair, and other Scandinavian design was "human and warm . . . personal, national, and universal."[45] Gordon's version of Scandinavian design was a projection of her ideal vision of what American design could be, and what America itself should be.

Gordon's claims were part of a broader period discourse that presented the home as a Cold War battlefield. At trade fairs and exhibitions overseas, the United States exhibited model homes fully outfitted with modern appliances and furniture as propaganda to sell the American way of life—most famously in 1959, when a model home at the American National Exhibition in Moscow served as the stage set for Richard

Nixon and Nikita Khrushchev's Kitchen Debate, in which the American vice president and the Soviet premier debated the merits of capitalism and communism. Gordon's arguments in the pages of *House Beautiful* similarly politicized design for American readers, implying that to buy a Wegner chair was to invest in America's democratic future. The stories she told to politicize the furniture advanced her own design agenda, and may have refracted back onto those told by Danish sellers.

In 1957, two years before *House Beautiful* published an issue on Scandinavian design, Asger Fischer and Gordon corresponded and arranged to meet during Fischer's upcoming, month-long trip to America. Fischer would later be celebrated for, in the words of Den Permanente's chairman, Aage E. Jensen, "energetic promotional efforts" that gave shape to the special issue.[46] But it seems the influence ran both ways. After returning home, Fischer would begin telling a story that linked Danish design to the Cold War.

In Fischer's anecdote, likely more parable than truth, a Danish cabinetmaker turns to craft to ease his fears of nuclear annihilation. "I come here to my workshop," the cabinetmaker says, "and I work on this chair. The world is mad, but this chair is sane. Notice when the Danish beechwood and the Bangkok teakwood come together; see the grains, feel the surface, look at the curve of that back—that will be a good chair. When I have finished it, I can feel proud of my work. I shall have made something sound and honest, and it will last."[47] Craft, Fischer's story suggests, offered the cabinetmaker tangible comfort amid the Cold War's existential threat.

In Gordon's *House Beautiful* editorials, the honesty and human touch invoked by Fischer's parable were not simply principles of craftsmanship. They were political principles that affirmed an American national identity even as they were used to upbraid an American design industry characterized by what Gordon deemed a lack of freedom on the part of the designer, who "designs for the professionals like himself—not for the buying public."[48] Scandinavian design, by contrast, was design for the people, never mind that pieces like the Chieftain and the Chair were too expensive for most buyers or that many Danes continued to fill their homes with neoclassical-style furniture.

Gordon's colleague Marion Gough suggested that Danish furniture carried this democraticness in its form. In an article celebrating Wegner as "the greatest world influence on furniture design," she highlighted the Chair as his breakthrough design and underscored how quickly audiences embraced it.[49] "Early in 1950," she wrote, "we observed with our own eyes how tourists in Den Permanente in Copenhagen singled it out in this shop where all things are beautiful, how they stood and delighted in the sight of it. . . . We heard people say that this was the kind of 'modern' they liked."[50] Perhaps she was offering a truthful recollection. Gough had visited Den Permanente in the summer of 1950 for an article about a Scandinavian sojourn.[51] But she was offering more than a memory. She was making an argument for the Chair as a piece of democratic design. "In retrospect," she reflected, "it is a significant part of the Wegner story that people were 'discovering' this beauty even before the experts stamped it with their approval."[52] It was not only, as Gordon proposed, the structure of the Danish design industry that was democratic; democracy was, claimed Gough, a feature of the designed objects that came out of it, as evidenced by their popular appeal.

George Tanier, an American importer of Danish design with a shop on New York City's tony Madison Avenue, used this idea as the premise of an advertising campaign that ran in the *New Yorker* beginning in 1958 (fig. 3.5). Each ad featured a Danish expatriate, a piece of furniture, and a testimonial quote. The quotes begin uniformly: "My name is Yvonne Morange. I am a Dane," says a young woman sitting in a chair designed by Arne Vodder. "My name is Per Sabroe, I am a Dane," says a young man wearing a three-piece suit and leaning against a Hans Wegner cabinet. A few of the Danes mention their professions. One is a product design consultant, another a secretary. All close their statements by affirming the quality of Tanier's imports. "I think that George Tanier's selections of Danish furniture and lighting represent the best things coming out of Denmark today," recite three of them, word for word. The others offer variations on the same theme. In all of the ads, ordinary Danes laud the furniture, suggesting that the nonspecialist is as comfortable and capable of evaluating its design as the expert. The message was clear: Danish design was a design of the people. It was, in other words, demo-cratic and, perhaps more importantly for the purposes of the campaign, accessible to the masses.

In fact, however, while high-end and midtier American shelter and lifestyle magazines lauded Wegner's work, their Danish counterparts rarely did. *Tidens Kvinder* (Today's Woman), a Danish fashion magazine that regularly published articles on dwelling culture, seldom highlighted the Chieftain, the Chair, or any of the other furniture known in the United States as Danish design. Its interiors were instead staged with overstuffed floral armchairs and dressers modeled on nineteenth-century French ones.[53] Furniture by the likes of Juhl and Wegner was advertised not there but in *Bygge og Bo* (Build and Live), a far more exclusive culture magazine concerned as much with modern art as with modern design. The Chieftain, the Chair, and other furniture that American tastemakers presented to consumers as objects of everyday life in Denmark—designs

"My name is Inge Andersen, I am a Dane. I come from the city of Hadsten. In the United States I am a secretary to a Danish executive. I have seen George Tanier's selections of Danish furniture and lighting and I would say without hesitation, that they are certainly representative of the best things being made in Denmark today.

GEORGE TANIER INC

521 Madison Ave., New York 22, N. Y.
Through dealers, decorators, architects

Rocker by Hans J. Wegner

Figure 3.5
Advertisement for George Tanier Inc., ca. 1958. © Nanna Tanier.

that "even the poorest Dane can afford," as a journalist wrote in the *Cincinnati Post*—were, in reality, rarefied.[54]

Tastemakers deployed Danish design as a marker of democratic American values, fitting it into a field defined, as Juhl relayed, by the popular industry slogan "American furniture for American citizens."[55] Whether or not the assertion of Danish/American likeness was why consumers bought the furniture, it penetrated their impression of Danish design and of Denmark more broadly. Doris Scherbak, for example, told Fischer that her American friends in Paris preferred to hire Scandinavian cleaning women. "I suppose because so few Americans speak French well enough to manage with French help," she speculated. "But also because the Scandinavian girls are more used to doing things as we do things."[56]

Consumers

In late May 1954, shortly after Doris Scherbak and her family moved their Danish things into their new, American-style apartment, she wrote again to Fischer, this time to tell him how happily they were settling in. "The furniture was delivered to our new apt. just a few days after we moved in," she told him, "and all our neighbors are quite envious of our things, especially the desk and the teak tables."[57] It's easy to read her satisfaction, which she would reiterate two years later, when she wrote to Fischer of another admirer. "We are so enjoying all our Danish things, I wish you could see them in our house," she began:

> A woman nearby who had passed often stopped by and asked if she
> could come in and look at our furniture as she said she had looked at it

so often through the large front window and was dying to see the rest of it. We have the loveseat with its back in front of the window and it certainly must be tempting to those who don't know it from the front.[58]

In both letters, Scherbak writes of admiring neighbors as an affirmation of her own good taste and also, at least in part, as a way to compliment Fischer. Not only do Scherbak and her family enjoy the things from Fischer's store; simply passing by her home, others fall for them too.

Scherbak was one of many Den Permanente shoppers who wrote Fischer with compliments on the store's wares. Rosalie S. Fasolu adored her "exquisite" Hingelberg silver, "the most beautiful in the world."[59] Tourist Cyra Sanborn, writing from Stockholm, where she was looking to buy furniture and ceramics, longed to return to Denmark and, parroting the marketing narrative, its fine craftsmanship. "The only furniture here that we've truly admired," she told Fischer, "has been a teakwood dining room set . . . by Finn Juhl!"[60] And from his home in Hopewell Junction, New York, David Greenberg wrote that the Danish furniture he and his wife, Marian, bought "continues to excite admiration and we are more and more pleased with it."[61]

As significant as the themes of their admiration—Danish design's beauty, craftsmanship, and ability to inspire envy—is that all of these Americans wrote to Fischer in the first place. This was not simply because Fischer was a gregarious personality and a good correspondent, though he does seem to have been both. It was also because he actively cultivated friendships with clients. On a trip to the United States in 1957, he filled his itinerary with jaunts across the country to see people who had bought furniture from him. "The schedule is rather tight as Den Permanente has asked me to pay visits to a lot of our customers," he wrote in a letter to Elizabeth Gordon.[62] For Fischer, this was good business. He understood that to sell the Chieftain, the Chair, and other Danish design was not just a matter of furnishing an attractive store with useful services. It required social relationships.

Fischer's address book was full of American names. He corresponded with professors and doctors, design editors and department store owners, Supreme Court justice Harold Burton and philanthropist Paul Mellon. While some had an evident professional interest in Danish design, others were casual customers of Den Permanente, people who had visited Copenhagen on vacation and bought a piece of jewelry or a chair. Most of Fischer's correspondents were white, wealthy professionals (or their wives). They were members of America's elite class, the sort of people who might subscribe to *House Beautiful* and visit, or even sit on the boards of, institutions like the Wadsworth Atheneum, the Art Institute of Chicago, and other museums that hosted *Design in Scandinavia*. This never came up in the correspondence, but it served as the backdrop to exchanges of pleasantries and travel plans, price negotiations and confirmations that orders had been received. One buyer, an irrigation company executive, ordered a lamp and a chair without even knowing the price; another spent $333, nearly the price of a luxury, four-piece sterling coffee set from Danish silversmith Georg Jensen, to import a Chieftain with matching ottoman.[63] Though not all could spend quite so freely, most operated in circles of cultural privilege with access to education and travel. They did not know one another, but they constituted something of a taste community: they had in common their admiration and purchase of Danish design and, more concretely, through their correspondence with Fischer, a relationship with one of its purveyors.

Of course, not all who bought Danish design knew Fischer or shopped

Plate 1 Finn Juhl (designer), Niels Vodder (fabricator), Chieftain Chair, 1949. Teak and leather. Courtesy of Rago/Wright.

Plate 2 Hans Wegner (designer), Johannes Hansen (fabricator), Round Chair, 1949. Teak and cane. Courtesy of Rago/Wright.

Plate 3 (*facing page*) Finn Juhl, exhibition plan and elevation for Niels Vodder display, Cabinetmakers Guild Exhibition, 1949. Watercolor, pencil, and drawing ink on paper. Design-Museum Danmark. Photograph: Pernille Klemp.

GENNEMGANGS-STAND TIL SNEDKERLAUGETS MØBELUDSTILLING I KUNSTINDUSTRIMUSEET 1949. MAAL 1:20.
EN GREN, DER ER VASKET KUND REN OG HVID I STRANDKANTEN, HAR DEN FINE BLANDING AF STRUKTURENS KLARE OPBYGNING I VEKSTEN,
BEHANDLINGEN OG OVERFLADEN, SOM MAA VÆRE MAALET FOR MØBLET. DERTIL KOMMER STYRKEN, KONSTRUKTIONEN, OPFYLDELSEN AF
FUNKTIONSKRAVET.
ET SNEGLEHUS, EN GREN, AALABAG EN, MALERIET, SKULPTUREN, ET MØBEL - ALLE HAR DE FUNKTIONER AT OPFYLDE, MEN OGSAA
FANTASIEN OG FORMSPROGET ER FUNKTIONER. MATEMATIK ER ET FREMRAGENDE HJÆLPEMIDDEL, MEN IKKE ET MAAL.

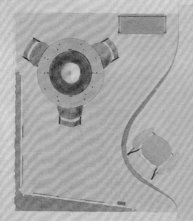

STANDEN SKAL MED SINE FORSKELLIGE BESTANDDELE FØRST OG FREMMEST VISE MØBLERNE, MEN I EN SAMMENHÆNG SOM KAN
FORKLARE OG UNDERSTREGE DERES FORM OG SAMMENHØRIGHED MED ANDRE KUNSTNERISKE FORETEELSER OG MED DE NATUR-
LIGE FOREKOMSTER, SOM INDTALER FANTASIEN OG UMIDDELBART LERER OG GLEDER VED FORMER, LINIER, FARVER, MATERIALER.
LOFT OG BAGVEG DEKKES AF STRIBET STOF FRA MARIE GUDME LETH. PODIET BEKLEDES MED BAGSTOF FRA WENBLER. SKULP-
TUR AF ERIK THOMMESEN, MALERIER AF BEN NICHOLSON, BORDLAMPEN AF GINO SARFATTI, ARMELUGE MILANO. PÅ DEMONSTRA-
TIONSSKÆRMENE FOTOGRAFIER, TEGNINGER, OBJEKTER, DER ILLUSTRERER OVENNEVNTE SYNSPUNKTER.

Plate 4 Finn Juhl (designer), Niels Vodder (fabricator), armchair (model NV-48), 1948. Stained teak and leather. Courtesy of Rago/Wright.

Plate 5 Finn Juhl, armchair for Baker, 1951. Watercolor on paper. DesignMuseum Danmark.
Photograph: Pernille Klemp.

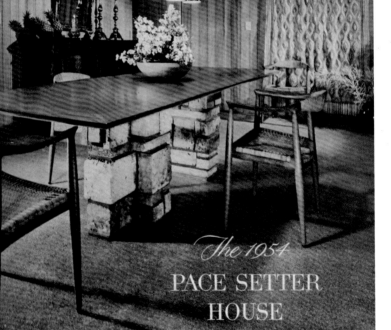

House Beautiful

NOVEMBER · 50¢

The 1954
PACE SETTER
HOUSE

Hans J. Wegner poet of practicality

A Danish designer with a genius for wedding lyricism to common sense is the world's greatest influence on furniture today

By MARION GOUGH

● In 1949 Hans J. Wegner, a soft-eyed, soft-spoken young man from Odense threw a significant pebble into the pool of furniture design. He created a chair—"The Chair," as it has since come to be known the world over. There was nothing startling or bizarre or experimental about it. It was unwrapped with no fanfare. But it had grace and freshness and, above all, a certain quality of truth which was sensed, as if intuitively, by people who never looked twice at furniture before.

Early in 1950, when The Chair was still unknown outside of Denmark, we observed with our own eyes how tourists in Den Permanente in Copenhagen singled it out in this shop where all things are beautiful, how they stood and delighted in the sight of it. They expressed wonder that wood uncoated by lacquer could be so smooth and satiny to the touch, how it could be molded so knowingly to conform to the human body. We heard people say that this was the kind of "modern" they liked, and there was lots of wistful American talk about the excellence of European craftsmanship. Later that year, The Chair was brought to the American market by Albert Hagemeyer of Watson and Basler in Chicago and by Georg Jensen. Although there were other Scandinavian designers, and good ones, working out of the same philosophy as Wegner, it seems to have been The Chair which first opened the world's eyes to the beauty of sculptured wood, rounded forms, and the *(Please turn the page)*

The practical design of "The Chair" makes it comfortable for dining, living-room sitting, or writing at a desk. Table by Wegner, Sofa fabric, Grundl. Rug designed by Sweden's Rittan Valberg for Cabin Crafts. Table is extendable, as you will see on page 78.

Plate 6 (*facing page*) *House Beautiful* cover, November 1953, featuring the 1954 Pace Setter House Dining Room with Hans Wegner's Round Chairs. © Ezra Stoller/Esto. Reprinted with permission of House Beautiful © 1953.

Plate 7 (*above*) *House Beautiful* spread, June 1959, featuring Hans Wegner's Round Chair. © Ezra Stoller/Esto. Reprinted with permission of House Beautiful © 1959.

UN-MATCHED BEAUTY: PINK AND RED. The mix is newer than the match, for lips, for fingertips.

A pink mouth and red nails—or the equally pretty vice-versa—is a summer Something.

Above: More mix-up: the harlequin bathing suit, by Tina Leser, in Heller wool jersey, $25; Lord & Taylor; Frost Bros.; I. Magnin.

Pink and red Martex beach towels. Dorothy Gray's "Portrait Pink" lipstick, "Sea Coral" nail polish, and Tanning Oil.

Opposite: Pink for the blouse—and her nails. Flame red for the skirt—and her lips. Over the almost-white foundation

on her eyelids, mauve-y shadow. Organdie blouse, pleated skirt of William Winkler nylon tulle, by Ceil Chapman, $90; Saks Fifth;

Montaldo's; The Dayton Co. Max Factor Hollywood "Clear Red No. 1" lipstick, his Pan-Stik and shadow on her eyes.

Plate 8 (*facing page*) *Vogue*, May 1951, featuring model Jean Patchett, seated cross-legged on a red towel at the beach. Clifford Coffin, Vogue, © Condé Nast.

Plate 9 (*above*) Axel Albeck display featuring furniture designed by Peter Hvidt and O. Mølgaard-Nielsen set against a wall painted in bright colors popular during the period, Cabinetmakers Guild Exhibition, 1951. DesignMuseum Danmark. Photographer unknown.

Plate 10 Finn Juhl, *Interior-52*, with Chieftain Chair in foreground, 1952, Nordenfjeldske Kunstindustrimuseum, Trondheim, Norway. Finn Juhl/US Copyright Office © 2022.

Plate 11 A photograph David Greenberg sent to Asger Fischer, showing Marian Greenberg in the couple's open-plan living/dining room. Items present include a ceramic plate by Richard Kjærgaard and a coffee table constructed of tiles by Lars Thursdlund. Hopewell Junction, New York, ca. summer 1954. Courtesy of the Greenberg/Freilich Family.

Plate 12 A photograph David Greenberg sent to Asger Fischer of David and Marian Greenberg's enclosed patio, with David Greenberg in Arne Vodder chaise lounge (ca. 1950) at left, Marian Greenberg on the right, and upholstered Ejner Larsen and Aksel Bender Madsen Metropolitan Chairs (1949) in the foreground. Hopewell Junction, New York, ca. summer 1954. Courtesy of the Greenberg/Freilich Family.

Plate 13 (*facing page*) Ad for Bassett Furniture Industry's "Danish-inspired" Tempo line, *Life*, 1962.

$???.??

What price Bassett's New TEMPO?

Furniture designed by Leo Jiranek, A.I.D., I.D.I.

Bedroom (upper left) costs you less than $250

Interior decoration by Nina Harrell

Dining room (upper right) is yours under $330

LESS THAN $250 FOR THIS FOUR-PIECE BEDROOM

BRING YOUR HOME BEAUTIFULLY UP TO THE MINUTE . . . with Tempo you can afford to! This sleek new group has a young look, an elegant manner. You'll treasure its slim, clean, Danish-inspired lines . . . in rich cherry veneer, as pictured, or walnut if you prefer. Both are finished with lasting DuPont Dulux®. Yet this double dresser with Pittsburgh Plate Glass mirror, bookcase bed, 4-drawer chest, and night table come to less than $250!■ Tempo lets you make up your own groupings, too . . . all so easy to own. Other bedroom pieces include a triple dresser, 8-drawer twin chest with mirror, a convenient desk. For your dining room, choose a rectangular, round, pedestal, or dropleaf table . . . with matching Formica® top if you like. Variety? Value? That's Tempo for you! See it and buy it, on budget terms, at your favorite furniture or department store. ■ Send 25¢ for Bassett furniture folders, table catalog, 16-page buyer's guide, to Bassett Furniture Industries, Dept. A2, Bassett, Virginia.

world's largest manufacturer of wood furniture

Bassett

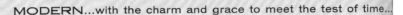

MODERN...with the charm and grace to meet the test of time...

Copenhagen

DANISH MODERN BY LANE

*Round Cocktail Table
with distinctive
four-piece matched top.
48" diameter, #862;
38" diameter, #863.*

*Drop Leaf Lamp Table . . . 22x24½x25½"
high, top opens to 22" x 40", #864*

*King-sized Cocktail Table . . .
72x17x15" high, #971*

*Picture Window
Table . . .
17x44x27½"
high, #860*

Lane designers have caught the very spirit of the age in Copenhagen . . . the celebrated collection of occasional tables that blends the new mood of soft grace with the fresh, clean lines of young modern. The wood is Softone Walnut, warmed to Lane's deep gleam finish. The lines flow and sweep upwards in continuing beauty. Twelve different styles—all with exquisite details, from the rounded contours framed and edged with beading to the molded stretchers pierced through tapered legs tipped with brass ferrules.

All over America young homemakers and families have found in Copenhagen the answer to taste and quality at modest prices. Lane also makes dining and bedroom furniture in the beautiful "Copenhagen" design. Write for free color brochure.

OVER 100 LANE TABLES, STARTING AS LOW AS $29.95
EASY TERMS AT MOST FURNITURE & DEPARTMENT STORES

THE LANE COMPANY, INC., ALTAVISTA, VA. IN CANADA: KNECHTELS, LTD., HANOVER, ONT.

LANE TABLES

BY THE MAKERS OF LANE CEDAR CHESTS AND LANE BEDROOM AND DINING ROOM FURNIT

Plate 14 (*facing page*) Ad for Lane Company's Copenhagen line, *Life*, 1958.

Plate 15 Verner Panton (designer), Fehlbaum and Co. (fabricator) for Herman Miller (distributor), Panton Chair, 1967. Molded plastic. Courtesy of Rago/Wright.

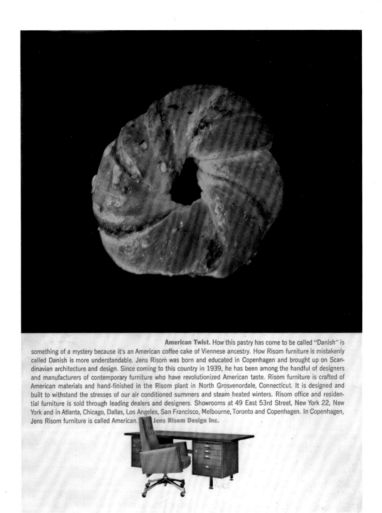

American Twist. How this pastry has come to be called "Danish" is something of a mystery because it's an American coffee cake of Viennese ancestry. How Risom furniture is mistakenly called Danish is more understandable. Jens Risom was born and educated in Copenhagen and brought up on Scandinavian architecture and design. Since coming to this country in 1939, he has been among the handful of designers and manufacturers of contemporary furniture who have revolutionized American taste. Risom furniture is crafted of American materials and hand-finished in the Risom plant in North Grosvenordale, Connecticut. It is designed and built to withstand the stresses of our air conditioned summers and steam heated winters. Risom office and residential furniture is sold through leading dealers and designers. Showrooms at 49 East 53rd Street, New York 22, New York and in Atlanta, Chicago, Dallas, Los Angeles, San Francisco, Melbourne, Toronto and Copenhagen. In Copenhagen, Jens Risom furniture is called American. **Jens Risom Design Inc.**

Plate 16 "American Twist," advertisement for Jens Risom Design Inc., *Interior Design*, 1961. Credit: Form Portfolios LLC.

at his store. One young couple from Baltimore bought their Chieftain from the Georg Jensen store in New York and placed it in the living room of a house designed by Marcel Breuer. As if to reconcile Elizabeth Gordon's opposition between Breuer's insidious modernism and Juhl's warm Scandinavian design, the Chieftain was placed next to tall sliding-glass doors, in full view of passersby, who, when the lights were on, might see its sculptural, bodily form framed by the geometric, glass and steel architecture. This act of placement—one might say, *display*—suggests again that members of Danish design's taste community were not fixed in their role as consumers. The Baltimore couple sited their Chieftain where neighbors could see it. Scherbak clearly appreciated how her loveseat appeared from the street, and her friends wanted Round Chairs for guests to both see and sit in. By bringing Danish furniture into their homes, they introduced others to it. Some were industry professionals whose job it was to promote design. Others arranged their Danish wares more casually, even so staging some to be seen by friends, colleagues, or passersby. Justice Burton, for instance, planned to display a pelican sculpture he had bought from Fischer among his law books, where he hoped its "pensiveness" would "communicate its message to those who see it . . . an inspiration to all who search for wisdom."[64] Remarking on the sheer quantity of Danish things he and his wife owned, David Greenberg, a writer on wildlife and conservation, sent photos and described both "the permanent show room of Den Permanente at my home" and the friends who enjoyed it (plates 11 and 12).[65] In thus displaying their things, Burton, Greenberg, and other American consumers of Danish design also did work akin to that of tastemakers.

David and Marian Greenberg formalized this role when, in 1954, they published the first of two regional retail handbooks, *The Shopping Guide* to Europe. (Their second, released the following year, was *The Shopping Guide to Mexico, Guatemala, and the Caribbean*.) In brief chapters organized by country, they advised readers where to go and what to buy. Of the seventeen pages on Denmark, more than half were dedicated to the goods on display at Den Permanente, and Fischer received a special note of thanks in the book's acknowledgments. Lela O'Toole, dean of the College of Home Economics at Oklahoma State University, annotated her copy with checkmarks, underlined items of interest, and, on a visit to Copenhagen, was sure to admire the Chieftain and the Chair during a visit to the famous store.[66]

In presenting furniture, the Greenbergs promised not a thorough account but "a 'spot' coverage to give the reader a general picture."[67] To this end, they highlighted a chaise lounge, an upholstered chair and ottoman, a teak dining table, teak end tables, an upholstered living room chair, a few sofas, and a Wegner writing table and chair. All were objects for the home, as opposed to the workplace, but there were no beds or vanities. The "general picture" offered to readers dealt primarily with the dining room and living room, where guests are entertained and the furniture is most likely to be seen. Chairs, pieces that may not only be viewed by guests but used by them, were given particular attention. The Greenbergs ended the section with the following instruction: "All you have to do is wait for the furniture to arrive and then call in the neighbors."[68] Themselves amateur tastemakers, the Greenbergs encouraged their consumer readers to take on a similar role.

The Greenbergs' work as amateur tastemakers extended beyond their shopping guide. David Greenberg was one of a few Fischer correspondents who recommended setting up a Den Permanente store in New York.[69] As early as 1948, another New Yorker, Rose van Sand, who dreamed up an export line called Denmark Originals that would ship Danish-made things to department stores across the US, proffered a similar idea: "a replica of your [Den Permanente's] building . . . near the Museum of Modern Art" to sell Danish design to Americans. She proposed just one variation from Den Permanente's Copenhagen layout, the addition of "a small, but perfect luncheon restaurant" on the top floor. A place to push an idea of Danishness through the menu—"*real* Danish sandwiches . . . you know—open sandwiches with only 1 piece of bread!"—it would also be, as a restaurant, a social space.[70] Nibbling on smørrebrød, patrons could dine with friends or clients while surrounded by Danish things. Van Sand's proposal conveyed a nuanced understanding of what it would take to popularize Danish design in the United States. Neither an appreciation of quality craftsmanship nor an identification with normative American values would alone be enough. Success would depend on building a taste community with real social bonds. Some, like those Fischer had with many of his clients, might be forged out of professional obligation. But others, like Scherbak's with her Parisian friends and with Fischer, with whom she sustained correspondence over many years, were more personally meaningful.

Though van Sand's plan for a New York Den Permanente never came to fruition, efforts like hers and David and Marian Greenberg's, along with the informal tastemaking of Doris Scherbak, Justice Burton, and others, suggest the ways in which consumers played different roles in the circulation of Danish design, facilitating its distribution not only by shopping but by mobilizing their social networks. The effect might be formally quantifiable (expanding sales channels) or far more informal— cultivating interest simply by displaying Danish design in their homes or offices. Knowingly or not, they practiced as amateurs alongside the

Figure 3.6 Still from the first televised presidential debate, featuring John F. Kennedy and Richard Nixon, with Hans Wegner's Round Chairs, 1960. Courtesy Getty Images, CBS Photo Archive.

professional tastemakers whose job it was to introduce Americans to the next design fad. They contributed to the rise in popularity of the Chieftain, the Chair, and other Danish design by exerting an influence that went beyond mere purchasing power.

: : :

In the autumn of 1960, Danish design received its largest audience yet when a pair of Wegner's Chairs shared the stage with nominees John

F. Kennedy and Richard Nixon in the first of their televised presidential debates—the first *ever* televised presidential debate (fig. 3.6). When Kennedy finished his opening remarks, he walked from the podium to his Chair and sat down, crossing his legs and settling in. When Nixon stood up to begin his, the Chair shared the screen with him for the first few moments, making it seem as though he was speaking not from a stage but from a sparsely decorated living room. Here was Danish design dressing the set of American political theater, furnishing the democracy on display as though it was the candidate best suited for the job. Making good on Gordon's claim about the democratic force of furniture, this broadcast would introduce Wegner's Chair and, by extension, Danish design, to sixty-six million Americans, more than a third of the population, far more than had ever shopped in Fischer's store, seen *Design in Scandinavia*, or read *House Beautiful*'s special issue on Scandinavian design. But it wasn't a design professional who selected the Chair to accompany Kennedy and Nixon on stage—it was a CBS executive who collected Danish design, a consumer who was also a tastemaker.

Mail Order Danish Modern

Given its many variants, it is ironic that in 1950s America, Hans Wegner's Round Chair came to be known as The Chair, a label emphatically singular. (By 1957 the nickname was common enough on both sides of the Atlantic that the Copenhagen store Den Permanente referred to the design as such in correspondence with American clients.[1]) Among the versions were the original design with its cane seat and wrapped back, a modification with cane seat and wooden back, and another with upholstered seat and wooden back. And then there were the copies—*House Beautiful* dubbed the Chair "the most stolen-from design in the world."[2] The Chair's minimal nickname reflected the design's iconic simplicity. Its crowning paradox is that the design's multiplicity, particularly in the form of knockoffs, was instrumental in popularizing it and Danish design more broadly. Low-quality knockoffs would transform Danish design from an esteemed brand into a recognizable style and reshape the cabinetmaker culture that had brought forth both the Chieftain and the Chair.

When American Doris Scherbak, the Danish design fan who outfitted her family's Paris apartment with furniture from Copenhagen, traveled to Mexico, she came home with two copies of Wegner's *klapstol* (or folding chair), an armless design from 1949, similar to the Chair in that it had a cane back and seat. She wrote that she was "happy to have the copies" and acknowledged the source of her pleasure: "They are really good copies and were so very cheap."[3] A good look and a cheap price—these features made copies enticing and Danish designers and fabricators anxious. They feared that copies would erode their market share and could, if poorly made, corrode the reputation for quality their exports enjoyed. But if copies deceived some buyers and caused certain dealers to rethink their distribution, they also helped build the market for Danish design *as a style* by permitting it to circulate more widely. In other words, the Chair was not only copied because it was popular, it was popular because it was copied.

Copies came in several varieties. Some imitated specific designs, like the *klapstols* Scherbak bought on vacation or the "outstanding" forty-dollar copies of "a popular Danish chair" that David and Marian Greenberg recommended to readers in their *Shopping Guide to Mexico, Guatemala, and the Caribbean*.[4] Others borrowed the general idea of Danish design. *House Beautiful* called these "copies which plagiarize the superficial form," and they were often realized as complete furniture suites.[5] "Almost all American furniture firms now have their 'Danish Line,'" reported *Life* magazine competitor *Look* in 1958.[6] Advertised as "Copenhagen Danish Modern" (Lane) "Danish-inspired" and "Royal Dane" (Bassett), and "truly Danish-Modern" (Stakmore), these American furniture sets borrowed certain features common among Danish imports—for example, all were made of wood—and codified them, helping to create a popular sense of Danish design and what it looked like. Copies of specific designs and of a general style allowed the idea of Danish design to circulate far more broadly than actual furniture from Denmark ever could. They also imbued it with a new character, one less controlled by sellers and tastemakers and less protectable by the Copenhagen-based cabinetmakers and *arkitekts* who had originated it.

Made in America

"If imitation is the highest form of compliment, Wegner has received it, for no designer's work is more brazenly copied," wrote Marion Gough in *House Beautiful* in 1959.[7] This was a bold claim in 1950s America, where design piracy was rampant and there were few legal protections to stop it. The problem was so serious that some manufacturers ceased production of specific designs entirely after other companies began producing cheaper versions. For example, shortly after Hans Knoll, founder of the furniture company Knoll, licensed the Hardoy (or Butterfly) chair from Argentinian designers Antonio Bonet, Juan Kurchan, and Jorge Ferrari-Hardoy, other companies began manufacturing an identical chair. When he sued for the unique right to manufacture, arguing that the copies misled consumers into thinking they were buying a chair made by his namesake company, the court ruled against him but instructed competitors to clearly label their versions. Inexpensive copies cut so far into Knoll's market that it was ultimately he who ceased production of the Hardoy. As the case of the Butterfly chair suggests, weak protections informed what manufacturers would produce. They also shaped how designers designed.[8]

In the United States at midcentury, furniture could be protected by two types of patents—utility or design. Utility patents offered protection for machines and other items that were deemed technologically novel and nonobvious, and that, because they were useful, were ineligible for copyright protection.[9] Objects of design did not typically fit the bill. A chair, for example, with four legs, a seat, and a back, was technologically conventional and obvious. Design patents, first made available in 1842, could protect furniture and other items, but only if they possessed applied ornament that was novel and nonobvious.[10] A chair, for example, could earn a design patent for its florid decorative detailing. To defend their products from piracy, midcentury American manufacturers sought to use these provisions by pushing designers to append superfluous decoration that would allow their work to be protected by design patents, or conceive more pared-down forms that were "technologically and materially innovative" and thus protectable by utility patents.[11] Still, copies proliferated.

In the United States, protections for usable goods like furniture were weak because Congress and the courts prioritized consumers' access to low-priced goods over the integrity of a designer's creation.[12] As one New York woman put it, "If a firm can make sufficiently good and cheap copies of Finn Juhl's or Hans Wegner's fabulously expensive chairs, then why should I, who admire the work of the architects (but who does not have a fabulous salary), not be able to get them?"[13] Both Juhl and Wegner had replies to this bid for increased access to their rarefied designs or, failing that, to pieces that resembled them.

Juhl called it "robbery."[14] Copies of his furniture entered the market almost as soon as his designs started selling in the United States.[15] But it was not only plagiarism of his own work that bothered him. Observing copies of Eames lounge chairs and Le Corbusier armchairs in New York furniture stores, he lamented the dishonesty. "I can understand if people are influenced by certain designs and try to do it better," he told the *New York Times* journalist who accompanied him on the shopping trip. "But they always go the other way and copy badly."[16] Juhl was drawing a distinction based on intention and quality. While his Danish colleagues may have modeled designs on recognizable referents—Kaare Klint's rocking chair based on a Shaker one, for instance—this, in Juhl's view, was not plagiarism but an attempt to improve upon the design (Klint modified the chair's top rail). Robbery was stealing the look of a recognizable design. It was copying a Chieftain and capitalizing on the resemblance.

Like Juhl, Wegner objected to copies, but his concern was more existential. "The curves have been copied too much without understanding," he told a reporter from *Interiors* in 1959. "A curve must have a meaning and a purpose. We did not set out to start a 'style' and now it is being overdone."[17] Wegner was making an argument for the functional significance of form and distinguishing it from mere looks. When he designed, for example, a folding chair that could be hung on the wall, the design included incisions in the frame from which the chair would hang. When an American company copied the chair, it was fixed rather than foldable but still had the incisions, now merely decorative.[18] Similarly, the Round Chair's curved back extending into arms permitted it to float atop its legs without a central vertical back support, thus serving a structural purpose. American manufacturers, however, used this sort of curve merely to invoke the idea of Danish design. They called it Danish Modern.

Previously, when the term "Danish Modern" had been used in Denmark, it was to describe furniture that served Danish taste and ignored American preferences.[19] What had come to be known as Danish Modern outside of Copenhagen's furniture scene and the individuals and institutions that constituted it was, by contrast, a look, geared toward American consumers and applicable to all sorts of home goods, from furniture to household appliances made by American companies. Electronics companies like Zenith offered a "Danish Modern style Lo-Boy" television cabinet called "The Nordic," and Magnavox sold its Debs Concert Grand Stereo Console in "six different wood finishes in three models, traditional, provincial, and Danish modern."[20] Even air conditioners (Westinghouse) and kitchen ranges (Hotpoint) could be sold in the style. Anything could be Danish Modern.

From the late 1950s into the 1960s, American furniture companies capitalized on the cachet of "Danish" to design and market their wares. Bassett, then one of the world's largest manufacturers of wood furniture, and other companies like Lane and Stakmore, a company specializing in folding chairs, released suites of furniture they called Danish (plates 13 and 14, fig. 4.1). Heywood-Wakefield produced two separate lines of Danish-inspired furniture, the first called Danish Casual (1959–1960) and the second Danish Modern (1960–1963). Contour, a maker of reclining lounge chairs, released a chair with "Danish modern styling," modifying its standard design by elongating the legs to accentuate their splay and separating the seat from the base so that it seemed to float (fig. 4.2). RCA Victor's Danish Modern Mark IX speaker cabinets featured sharp, squared-off corners and squat, tapered wooden legs (fig. 4.3). And alongside Kabuki decorator dolls, Samurai steak knives, and lacquerware serving dishes, Palley Supply Company offered *Ebony* readers a "Danish Style Imperial" armchair with seat and back cushions suspended from a boxy wooden frame (fig. 4.4). These examples highlight three of the features that, alongside wood and curves, came to define

The exciting experience of living modern . . . with Stakmore
folding chairs and tables. Here . . . tapered lines that are truly
Danish-Modern . . . a tawny walnut finish of pure elegance
(Or . . . choose wheat, fruitwood, mahogany or ebony finish, as you
prefer) . . . practical non-scuff Naugahyde upholstery in a brilliant
array of fashion colors. At fine stores everywhere or write:
STAKMORE CO. INC., 200 MADISON AVENUE, NEW YORK 16

Figure 4.1

Ad for Stakmore Company's
"truly Danish-Modern" line,
House Beautiful, 1956. Courtesy
MECO Corp.

Figure 4.2

Ad for three models of the
Contour Chair Lounge, including
Contoura, with "Danish modern
styling," *Esquire*, 1962.

Figure 4.3 Ad for RCA Victor's Danish Modern Mark IX stereo speaker cabinets, *Life*, 1959
Figure 4.4 Ad for Palley Supply Company, featuring "Danish Style Imperial" chair, *Ebony*, 1959.

the American knockoff version of Danish Modern: splayed, tapered, and floating forms.

Though these were common characteristics of the designs themselves, marketing highlighted a different detail: line. In ads, Bassett touted its furniture's "slim, clean, Danish-inspired lines," Lane offered "fresh, clean lines," and Stakmore sold "tapered lines that are truly Danish-modern." This emphasis was not new. It replicated language that Nordic journalists had used to talk about new design. Juhl, for example, was lauded for his "simplicity of line . . . ruthlessly reduced to a bare minimum." Sumptuous in its sparseness, his work was, critic Margarete Berger said, "a feast for the eyes."[21] The Chieftain commanded presence with its formidable size and profile, yet its structure was spare. The chair's lines were simple not only because they were unbroken by ornament, but also insofar as they showed the design's structure.

By contrast, American advertisements heralding line invoked recent fads in popular design. "Slim," "clean," "fresh," and "tapered"—the Danish-inspired suites fit right in with period modernism, to which ads and editorials attached similar adjectives, and seemed to promise an update of streamlined design.[22] Many designers and tastemakers condemned the streamlined style, which appropriated teardrop forms, developed to minimize friction in motion, for use in static objects like pencil sharpeners, toasters, and coffeepots. But in the 1930s and 1940s, streamlined design was preferred by American consumers, who filled their homes with furnishings and appliances made to look like they could move. While manufacturers liked that curved forms often strengthened materials, made machine production easier, and removed the risk of sharp corners getting chipped in transit, the popular taste for streamlining emerged from public education in the United States, which taught children the importance of good form and, also, how to recognize it.[23] For both organic machines, like bodies, and industrially manufactured ones, like cars, the goal was to be slender and sleek.[24]

That goal dovetailed with racializing discourses that used words like "vital" and "clean" to describe traits deemed desirable but not attributed to immigrants, for example, who were seen as deficient in hygiene.[25] Slim, clean, and tapered—the adjectives applied to American-made, Danish-styled furniture in ads placed in magazines with predominantly white readership, like *Life*—all built upon this ethos, if perhaps in a "fresh" variation. Though by the late 1950s the origins of such language may have been forgotten or, in the wake of the Holocaust, disavowed, selling the furniture in this way nonetheless presented Danish-styled furniture as a tool of assimilation. To buy a lounge chair or an air conditioner, the ads suggested, was to buy into white, middle-class norms.[26]

Attention to line also made its way into American editorials on Danish design. In *House Beautiful*, Marion Gough wrote that the "lyrical, fluid lines" of Wegner's Round Chair "take on the dimension of sculpture."[27] While Gough was discussing a particular Danish-made object by a particular Danish designer, similar language appeared in the pages of American popular magazines in reference both to design imported from Denmark and to American-made design that was styled after it. The two were thus cast as equivalent. Because far more people saw the furniture in print than did so in real life, this common language of line meaningfully shaped their sense of connection between Danish design from Denmark and American-made furniture in a so-called Danish style.

In fact, it was through photographic (and televisual) reproduction that most Americans became familiar with Danish design. When a set of four Wegner Round Chairs with cane seats and wrapped backs appeared in a photograph on the cover of the November 1953 issue of *House Beautiful*, copies were mailed out to at least half a million subscribers and more were sold at newsstands (see plate 6). An estimated 2.5 million people saw the Chair on that cover. By contrast, only 650,000 Americans saw the real thing on display in *Design in Scandinavia*. When, during that exhibition's three-year tour of North America, Johannes Hansen published a map plotting his workshop's sales, it showed shipments to seventy-four cities in twenty states; the majority, however, went to coastal shops and buyers.[28] Magazines with broad distribution (like *Popular Science*, which informed readers that knock-down innovations in Danish furniture simplified moving) and mailers with hyperlocal readership (like campus newspapers showing Danish tables and chairs furnishing new fraternity houses) disseminated Danish design far beyond the reach of the physical objects themselves.[29] Through outlets like these, reproduction in two dimensions dominated the American distribution of Danish design. There, on the page, articles and ads used "Danish" as an adjective to describe furniture from both Denmark and America. Instead of indicating affiliation to a country of origin or a specific tradition of manufacture within that country, it became a style. It became Danish Modern.

Danish-styled, American-made furniture became pervasive in part because it was so much more readily available for purchase than was furniture from Denmark. In the 1950s the Georg Jensen store in New York was the only stateside store to sell Niels Vodder–made Chieftains because its director, Frederik Lunning (namesake of the Lunning Prize, awarded annually to two Nordic designers), had, before his death in 1952, secured an exclusive distribution deal with the cabinetmaker. By contrast, Lane's "Copenhagen Danish Modern" line was available at furniture and department stores in towns and cities throughout America, a fact emphasized in the company's ads. Though Johannes Hansen had arrangements with multiple North American dealers, making the Chair more widely available than the Chieftain, it was still no competition for Lane's factory-made line. Production capacity continued to limit distribution, even after Hansen's workshop incorporated more mechanization. In 1957, when an American woman in Columbia, Missouri, sought to outfit her dining room with ten Round Chairs, she was told they wouldn't be delivered for a full year after receipt of the order.[30] By contrast, the thirteen million Midwestern recipients of the Sears Christmas catalog could make a toll-free call at any time of day to order a stereo in a Danish-style cabinet with splayed rounded legs and walnut veneer—and expect to receive it just a few weeks later.[31] Similarly, magazine readers who admired the Danish-inspired furniture pictured in Bassett's ads had the option of buying it in a local store or, for 25 cents, requesting a catalog and buyer's guide and then ordering a bedroom suite or dining set through the mail. Availability and accessibility made it easy for Americans to buy American-made Danish Modern.

American companies' factory-made, Danish-style design was also far cheaper than Danish design made in Denmark. The furniture was mass-produced for retail, with price tags to match. Lane's tables started at $29.95. Bassett's four-piece bedroom set, which included a double dresser, bookcase bed, four-drawer chest, and night table, cost less than $250, roughly the same as a pair of Round Chairs in leather and teak (the price changed depending on the materials) and less than a single Chieftain. Wegner's and Juhl's chairs, expensive to begin with—as one Danish *arkitekt* observed, the prices "are hardly what you would call 'democratic'"—were even pricier in the United States given shipping and other added costs.[32] Some American purveyors made the comparatively low cost of their wares a marketing tool; a brochure from the Tell City Chair Company in southern Indiana, advertising its Danish Modern set, touted prices "much lower than the imports."[33] Danish-styled, American-made furniture may have had little material connection to Denmark, but it was, as Doris Scherbak might have said, "ever so cheap" by comparison.

If the Chieftain was art, as Juhl claimed, and the Chair was an homage to the cabinetmakers, as said Wegner, Danish Modern style was for consumers. While Wegner and Juhl balked at the imitation Danish furniture, it flooded the market, as though making good on one of Danish design's key myths—that it was a furniture of the people. By the late 1950s, Danish Modern was everywhere—including Denmark.

Danish Copies

America was awash in copies, and Danish designers, fabricators, and other industry members were fearful. They perceived the threats posed by the copies already discussed: foreign-made knockoffs of popular designs, like the Wegner lookalikes Doris Scherbak bought in Mexico and the others that the Greenbergs recommended, and American design masquerading as Danish, typically in the form of "Danish Modern" furniture suites. These challenges were only getting worse. There were rumors of US manufacturers looking to poach Danish designers and Canadian firms hiring Danish émigré carpenters so that they could more credibly call their output Danish.[34] Replicas were coming not just from Mexico but from Yugoslavia and Taiwan.[35] And Japanese designers were reportedly set to flood the American market with their "Danish" furniture, at half the price of the real thing.[36] But particularly menacing was a third type of threat, which came from within: Danish-made knockoffs and low-quality furnishings in the Danish Modern style.

In 1955 the Danish tabloid *B.T.* reported on whispers of a plagiarism scandal at the annual Cabinetmakers Exhibition. Unfolding in a series of articles published in early October, just after the exhibition opened, the story focused on a folding chair Preben Thorsen had designed for cabinetmaker Jacob Kjær, and accused Thorsen of pirating a Wegner design Johannes Hansen had shown alongside the Chair at the 1949 exhibition.[37] (That Kjær, then the exhibition's spokesperson, had opened the show by remarking upon the threat of copies made the charge even sharper.[38]) Though both Hansen and Wegner expressed surprise at the two chairs' resemblance, Wegner refuted the accusation by pointing to a handful of subtle differences. For one, his chair was upholstered in goat-skin and Thorsen's was not. In any case, Wegner said, Thorsen had been a student of his at the School of Arts and Crafts in Copenhagen (where Wegner, too, had trained)—as if to suggest it was only natural that students model their work after their instructors'.[39] (Thorsen, meanwhile, answered the charge by passing the buck; the plans he had drawn, he claimed, proposed a chair very different from Wegner's, but Kjær had altered the design in the fabrication process.[40]) *B.T.*'s allegation may have been inflated—none of Denmark's other major dailies ran the story—but by insisting that plagiarism had infiltrated even the Cabinetmakers Exhibitions, the paper amplified a growing paranoia about how copies might destroy the Danish furniture industry from the inside.

The concern, as expressed in the press and documented in the minutes of Cabinetmakers Guild meetings, typically centered on the fact that manufacturers in Denmark, capitalizing on the fad for Danish, had begun exporting shoddy goods that threatened to undercut sales of quality Danish design and compromise its reputation abroad. The craftsmen were right to worry. In the late 1950s, Danish journalists reported rumors of American dealers discontinuing distribution of products with the "Danish" label because it was no longer the guarantee of quality it had been even a few years prior. "It is bad when Americans copy us," observed the director of the manufacturer France and Søn, "but, is worse when Danish producers copy each other."[41]

That *B.T.*'s story involved a copy of a Wegner design was hardly inci-

Ting, der ligner . . .

Things wich look like . . .

Spisestol fra »Tidens Møbler« 1957

Dining-chair from the exhibition »To day's Furniture« 1957

Detail af spisestol tegnet 1952 af Hans J. Wegner

Detail of a dining-chair designed in 1952 by Hans J. Wegner

Figure 4.5a Detail of a dining chair from the exhibition *Tidens Møbler* (1957) alongside detail of a dining chair designed by Hans Wegner (1952), *Mobilia*, November/December 1957. Photographer unknown.

dental. In Denmark, as elsewhere, his furniture was a frequent target of piracy. At the 1957 *Tidens Møbler* (Today's Furniture) exhibition staged at the Tivoli amusement park, a Danish manufacturer proudly displayed a version of a Wegner dining chair from 1952; the copy borrowed the fishtail curve of Wegner's original seat back but flattened it somewhat, not producing an exact replica (fig. 4.5a). As an article in *Mobilia* pointed out, this was one of many knockoffs on display. Another took its form, joinery, and dimensions from a design by furniture *arkitekt* Hans Olsen, elongat-

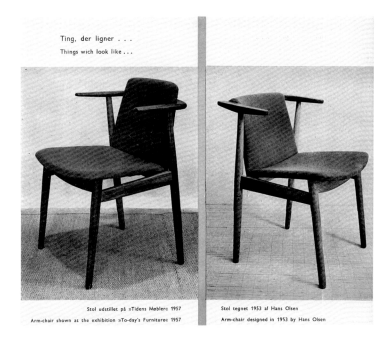

Figure 4.5b Armchair from the exhibition *Tidens Møbler* (1957) alongside armchair designed by Hans Olsen (1953), *Mobilia*, November/December 1957. Photographer unknown.

ing the backrest and flattening the taut, wrap-around arms in its only gestures at variation (fig. 4.5b). Just a few blocks away, Den Permanente sold the real thing. But staged among Tivoli's twinkle lights, carousel, and promenades, *Tidens Møbler* offered copies that looked nearly as good for a fraction of the price. And when exported to America, both the real thing and the copy were legitimately labeled "Made in Denmark."

In response to the growing industry of Danish-made copies, cabi-netmakers and manufacturers experimented with ways of marking their furniture. In 1959 a group of manufacturers, prompted by American dealers, who wanted the quality of the furniture they sold guaranteed, formed the Danish Furnituremakers' Control Association, developing industry standards and labeling furniture that met them with a small black logomark designed by Wegner—one of his few forays into graphic design—that read "Danish Furnituremakers Control." Participating furniture makers—by 1963 there were about sixty—submitted to at least six months of factory and product inspections in exchange for use of the seal to authenticate the quality of the furniture they exported.[42] Cabinetmakers and manufacturers also developed markings to certify their individual brands.

Fabricators found different ways of marking their designs. Some used stamps, printing on the surface of the wood with ink. Johannes Hansen tried nailing metal labels to the underside of the Round Chair and the other designs turned out by his workshop; other makers also adopted this practice. For the Chieftain, Niels Vodder favored branding the wood with a hot iron, leaving a dark impression burned into the material's surface. Johannes Hansen also used this method, and many viewed it as the most effective marking because it was "difficult—if not impossible—to remove it."[43] This, proponents argued, might make it harder to pass off a replica as the real thing.

Such markings, linking a piece of furniture to a specific maker, were directly derived from observations of the American market, where furniture was often labeled with a designer or manufacturer's name. Distributors found that when Danish furniture was likewise connected to a specific individual or company, it sold better.[44] The markings, a declaration of that connection, also served to distinguish a particular maker's goods from those by other designers and manufacturers, and from unbranded wares hawked by supply companies. An American importer of Danish furniture confirmed the value of logomarks for producers—unlike furniture designs, they were protectable under law—and their usefulness for consumers, who could use them to identify a "genuine product." But the markings, the importer pointed out, would only be effective if accompanied by "a comprehensive advertising campaign so that the purchasers know what to look for."[45] As it was, ads rarely included illustrations of logomarks because the importers and dealers who placed them were typically emphasizing *their* brand (George Tanier or John Stuart, for example). They tended to highlight a specific piece alongside the name of the maker or, more commonly, the designer, set in large block letters for graphic clarity but with no illustration of or connection to the maker's specific mark. Though this may have cultivated name-brand recognition, it didn't deter copies. In fact, it spurred knockoffs. The Danish company that copied Wegner's dining chair with its fishtail curve and the Mexican ones that made their own versions of his folding, Round, and other chairs capitalized on the iconicity of the designs and their association with the designer. This is also what attracted Doris Scherbak. She knew they weren't real, but they looked like they were. Even though they were copies, she felt as if she had added a pair of Wegners to her collection of Danish design.

For Wegner, this was a problem. In 1959 he appealed to Denmark's Maritime and Commercial Court to secure copyright for two iterations of the Chair, the 501 with the woven or solid back and woven seat, and the 503 with the solid back and upholstered seat. His attorneys built the case on a Danish legal provision established in 1908 that permitted design to be covered by copyright. Useful objects like chairs were not automatically granted copyright but could be awarded it on a case-by-case basis, according to guidelines that had been developed to evaluate art. The provision charged judges with evaluating a designer's artistic talent and an object's aesthetic capacity based on expert testimony. Wegner's Chair was a strong contender for acquiring protection; when Mogens Koch, a furniture *arkitekt* and professor of furniture in the School of Architecture at the Royal Danish Academy of Fine Arts, took the stand and called the Chair a "marked example" of an "original work of art," his testimony could be supported by a decade's worth of international journalism, marketing, and accolades celebrating it as such.[46] Lawyers were able to present articles, like one from *Industrial Design* in which Edgar Kaufmann Jr. referred to Wegner as "an artist"[47]; advertisements, like one circulated by a Brooklyn department store that called the design "pure sculpture in wood"; and a history of display in art museums, such as during the *Design in Scandinavia* tour. All served as evidence of the aesthetic originality Wegner deployed when designing the Chair, and the court ruled in his favor. Wegner won copyright protection for his Chair.

The ruling set an important precedent, prompting the Danish Parliament to approve new protections for useful objects, including furniture. The Copyright Act of 1961 protected originator's rights (*Ophavsret*) by recognizing originality far more capaciously than before. It specified that a design object "ought to be protected without taking into account its practical purpose."[48] In practical terms, this meant that a chair was no longer disqualified simply because, like other pieces that served a similar function, it had a seat, a back, and four legs. The law recognized design, like literary and artistic work, as the product of "personal," "creative," and "independent" conception, and promised to protect it as such.[49]

The new law's teeth were soon tested. When a Finnish manufacturer sued a Danish one for copying the distinctive grooved handles on a set of flatware designed by Finn Kaj Franck, experts appointed by the Danish court argued that, although the grooves in the Danish flatware may not have been original, their "overall effect" was.[50] Though Franck's design was unambiguously protected by the recent copyright act, the particular motif was not new and thus could be reproduced without fault. This argument carried the day, setting a dangerous precedent in which copyright applied only to the "total artistic effect achieved by the presentation and juxtaposition of details."[51] If originality lies in the overall effect, arguably a copy that is similar but not identical could produce a different overall effect. How could designers defend or protect something as amorphous as "effect"?

Before the new law was passed, a reporter who had visited Tivoli and seen the rampant piracy on display at *Tidens Møbler* wrote that copies made the designer feel "that he was the victim of a robbery. But he could not address himself to the police, because the police did not take care of that kind of robbery."[52] This changed after Wegner's lawsuit and the Copyright Act of 1961. But because of the emphasis on effect, it remained difficult and expensive for designers to prove that a robbery had even occurred. A defendant might argue, for instance, that flattening the fishtail curve in a chair's seat back was enough to alter the overall effect of the design.

When cabinetmaker Johannes Hansen, Wegner's longtime collaborator, testified in the case of Wegner's Chair, he had voiced skepticism about design's ability to stand up to a concept of originality akin to that which defined art. He did not believe, he told the court, that "a chair, which is an object of everyday use for lots of people, and which is, in advance, made for such a use, and which can be made by any decent cabinet maker, and which to a large extent looks like any other chair, could be considered as an original work of art."[53] Furniture, he suggested, was reproducible; was free of any unique, gestural maker's touch; and tended to resemble other pieces of a similar type. Not only do chairs tend to have a seat, a back, and four legs, but particular types—like spindle chairs, with their slender rods running vertically up the back like a comb, or folding chairs, with their low, light frames—draw upon historical styles and thus bear close resemblance to their predecessors and to one another. Given all of this, how could features used to establish a work of art as original be transferred to design?

A chair designed by Verner Panton the year after Wegner filed his lawsuit offers one answer. Panton, like Juhl, had studied architecture at the Royal Academy of Art, and his Panton Chair, a brightly colored, S-shaped plastic chair that seems to swim up out of the floor, departs from Hansen's characterization of furniture in every way (plate 15). First, though it was developed in 1960, it was not widely released until 1967; at least initially, then, it was not available for widespread use. Second, early versions of the chair were painted from top to bottom, like a canvas, potentially bearing the gestural mark of the painter's hand. Third, and perhaps most importantly, Panton's design didn't look like other chairs. Made of a single piece of plastic, it had no legs but rather a base that served as a seamless extension of seat and back. In all of these ways, the Panton Chair is a design object that fits the parameters of originality established for works of art. Though it is a far cry from the Danish design born out of the Cabinetmakers Exhibitions and popularized in the 1950s, it might be thought of as one form of reaction to the copy culture, a way of protecting design from the rampant piracy that preoccupied other designers and fabricators. Panton's design suggested the industry move in a radical new direction, embracing new materials, technologies, and forms. But could a design community that had established its international reputation on traditional materials (like wood), craftsmanship, and modern takes on classic types endure or even tolerate such a transformation?

Keeping Up with the Copies

Copies made it difficult to pin down exactly what constituted Danish design. Was it furniture designed in Denmark? Or did it have to be made there too? What about furniture made in America that called itself Danish? The confusion owed not only to reproduction but to varied arrangements between Danish and American companies. *House Beautiful* succinctly explained the nuance to its readers: some furniture "is imported in toto; some is partially made abroad and assembled in American factories; some is made here from designs created in Scandinavia."[54] In some cases, a single company distributed furniture fitting more than one of these categories. The American manufacturer Selig, for example, both assembled Danish designs that had been partially made abroad *and* imported finished furniture, which it marketed with a distinctive round label that read "Made and Finished in Denmark" atop the Danish flag's white cross on a red field. As affiliation with Denmark came to signal cachet, it also, simultaneously, became a mark of confusion. Just as the furniture industry's effort to expand into the American market had directed design styles and reshaped production methods in the decade after World War II, so too would this culture of copies and responses to it radically transform the work of the cabinetmakers and the *arkitekts* with whom they partnered.

The designer Jens Risom took advantage of the simultaneity of cachet and confusion around Danish design in a 1961 ad campaign called "American Twist," which ran in trade periodicals like *Interiors* and popular magazines like the *New Yorker* (plate 16). Featuring a large image of a pastry above a block of text and a thumbnail of a Risom-designed desk and chair, the ad compared Risom furniture, "mistakenly called Danish," to the Viennese-inspired American pastry known as a Danish. Though the text acknowledged that in Risom's case the "Danish" descriptor was "more understandable" (and, to capitalize on the fad, made sure to mention that he'd been "born and educated in Copenhagen and brought up on Scandinavian architecture and design"), it mainly poked fun at the label as a meaningless descriptor assigned to things, like the donut-shaped pastry, that had little true connection to Denmark.

Later, in 1968, the US Federal Trade Commission ruled that the loose application of "Danish," like that which Risom's ad simultaneously sent up and deployed, deliberately misled consumers and thereafter prohibited its use for any item not manufactured in Denmark. "If it's called 'Danish,' 'Danish modern' or 'Danish designed,' it must have been made or designed in Denmark," explained a personal finance magazine in 1969, relaying the FTC's decision to its readers. "Imitations made elsewhere can be called 'Danish manner' or 'Danish style' just as long as the furniture follows traditional Danish lines," it continued, echoing the concern for line long highlighted by American manufacturers.[55] Danish, once an adjective that signaled quality, no longer carried definite meaning but instead received its meaning from the term it modified. "Danish modern" or "Danish designed" connected furniture to its nation of origin, while "Danish manner" or "Danish style" attached it to a look codified through many and varied copies.

These copies invented Danish style as much as they borrowed from it. And this invention both spread the taste for Danish in the US and shaped what furniture makers in Denmark put into production. Though publicly the press would declare that "the special characteristic of Danish furniture" had neither to do with "the use of a particular kind of wood, nor a particular type [of] chairleg," behind the scenes, fabricators were pressured to hew to a certain picture of Danish design held by the popular press and the public.[56] For example, after fabricating prototypes of a molded aluminum chair designed by Poul Kjærholm (who trained as a cabinetmaker, worked for a time with Hans Wegner, and would go on to teach in the furniture department at the Royal Academy), manufacturer Chris Sørensen decided not to put it into production because distributors had objected that it was not "distinctively Danish."[57] Perhaps the problem was the material (metal rather than wood) or the chair's shape (like a folded oval), or perhaps its legs did not present a legibly Danish line. Even as Danish fabricators sought to protect their designs from the rampant copies, they found themselves subservient to the expectations produced by those copies.

This became increasingly evident as the market for Danish furniture continued to expand. The growth was rapid. During the first seven months of 1960, for example, exports were up 50 percent from the same period the prior year.[58] Publicly, this was celebrated, including at Den Permanente, where the shop's walls showed illustrated graphs detailing the increase in Danish domestic cultural export over the past decade.[59] But internally, confidence wavered as to whether such growth could be sustained.[60] While some, like cabinetmaker Johannes Hansen, advocated for ramping up production but limiting circulation to a small number of dealers so as to sustain the furniture's desirability through its rarefied status, others saw opportunity only in growth.[61] Many thought that even to hold exports steady, *arkitekts* would need to churn out new designs, and makers to get them into production, more quickly.[62] This was not only a matter of enticing foreign buyers with the promise of the new, a practice already well established in the United States and characteristic of consumer culture more broadly. It was also a way to stay ahead of the copies. If new designs just kept coming, by the time the knockoffs hit the market, they'd be but dated reproductions of last year's models.

But prioritizing new designs would radically change the industry, in that furniture makers could no longer rely on their back catalog. Instead of cabinetmakers and manufacturers making long-term investments in designs they might fabricate year after year, perhaps with minor modifications, the new system required rapid turnover and constant novelty. They would have to invest in innovation each season, giving over materials, manpower, and machines to new models. This would only be viable with production runs larger than most furniture makers could dependably sell in a season. Not even the ballooning retail market could guarantee seasonal sales large enough to compensate for the investment. It is perhaps no coincidence, then, that at the turn of the 1960s, the industry turned to office furniture, where large orders were more likely.

The fate of Juhl's furniture for the American furniture company Baker seemed to forecast the reorientation toward the workplace. Originally marketed for domestic spaces under the name Baker Modern, it was rebranded in 1958, when the company folded the line into its "Modern Group," as "particularly appropriate for the environment of a V.I.P."[63] The Chieftain, too, which Juhl said he had conceived as a comfortable reading chair, was repurposed as an office chair, dressing Danish consulates and Scandinavian Airlines (SAS) ticket offices around the world.

(To imbue the design with a more formal, professional air, the seventy-eight consulate-destined Chieftains were done in dark rosewood rather than bright teak.)

If Juhl's shift to the office evinced a push to develop new markets for existing designs, Wegner's sparked a new design trajectory. He began deliberately focusing his attention on furniture for institutional settings and experimenting with new materials to suit the spaces. For example, in the 1960s, Wegner collaborated with the manufacturer Getama to design furniture for student dorms and nursing homes—both of which lent themselves to high-volume sales—and revisited wood laminates, a strong yet malleable layered composite he had first explored in the late 1940s. Back then, in submissions to the Museum of Modern Art's competition inviting new designs for low-cost furnishings, he had proposed a number of pieces, including three different shell chairs, each of which would be stamped out of a single sheet of plywood and then pressed into shape. None of the chairs won the competition, and, requiring special machines to fabricate, they never went into production. (A watercolor rendering of one of the designs was, however, included in a publication about the competition, yet another instance of Danish design circulating through reproduction. Years later, for an exhibition, Wegner would produce a full-scale model of it to prove that fabrication was possible.[64]) Wegner remained interested in laminates beyond the competition, though manufacturing costs were prohibitive. For example, the Tri-Partite Shell Chair of 1949 was so expensive to fabricate—largely because Hansen's workshop was forming it by hand rather than using machines to stamp and mold the plywood—that it was only ever available by special order.

In 1963, after Johannes Hansen's death, Wegner returned to laminate in the Two-Part Shell Chair, designed in partnership with the cabinetmaker's foreman, Nils Thomsen. The simplified, two-dimensional curves of its angled back and its seat, which swings up so dramatically that in the US the design became known as the Smiling Chair, made its production more straightforward. Machine assistance would make it even easier. But the machine was expensive. For it to be economical, Johannes Hansens Møbelsnedkeri (as the company was then called) would have had to produce and sell at least ten thousand Smiling Chairs, which risked tipping the company from craft enterprise into a business that more closely resembled large-scale manufacturing. Though before his death Hansen had confessed to "rationalizing" his production—a euphemism for introducing some machinery to scale up production—he was insistent that his workshop remain craft-based at its core.[65]

The case of the Smiling Chair reveals the difficulty of staying ahead of the copy market. Doing so would require material innovation and large-scale runs, but the craft industry on which Danish design had built its brand could support neither. As copies afforded widespread access to Danish style, the cabinetmakers sought to keep up. Borrowing the production techniques of the manufacturers from whom they sought to distinguish themselves, their industry was transformed in the process. Though copies sowed buyer confusion and ate into the retail market, it was ultimately the industry's own efforts to combat these threats that fundamentally transformed the culture and ethos of the Danish design made famous in the 1950s.

: : :

In 1966 the Danish Cabinetmakers Guild held its fortieth and final annual exhibition. Visitor numbers had decreased, and the exhibition's longtime organizer, Poul Christiansen, had stepped down. By the early 1960s,

Figure 4.6 Johannes Hansen display featuring furniture designed by Hans Wegner, Cabinet-makers Guild Exhibition, 1966.

many cabinetmakers, including Johannes Hansen, had begun prioritizing their own showrooms over exhibition participation.

For this final show, Hans Wegner designed conference room furniture for Johannes Hansens Møbelsnedkeri (fig. 4.6). Juhl was nowhere to be seen. His adieu to the exhibition that had launched his career as a

Figure 4.7 L. Pontoppidan display featuring furniture designed by Finn Juhl, Cabinetmakers Guild Exhibition, 1965.

furniture designer had come the year before, in 1965, when he designed office furniture for cabinetmaker L. Pontoppidan (fig. 4.7). (His regular partnership with Niels Vodder had deteriorated some years earlier, and more formally broke apart in 1966 when Vodder told Juhl that he no longer wished to produce his furniture.[66] In 1971 Vodder ceased production of Juhl's furniture altogether, the Chieftain included.) Absorbing the characteristic tenets of Danish style, as codified by American copies, the desk chair Juhl designed for the second-to-last Cabinetmakers Exhibition featured legs that were swollen and splayed and a seat back that seemed to float. At least that's how it appeared from the front. Viewed from the back, it was the seat that seemed to float, whereas the chair back appeared awkwardly affixed to a curved rail with short arms that looked like a stunted take on Wegner's Round Chair. The desk it accompanied was also upholstered, its top covered in a silky caramel leather "so delicate," one critic wrote, "that even someone who never uses a pen or other writing utensil, and who would only use it as a place to sit and think would be distracted by his fear of staining it."[67] This suite, the leather desk covering seemed to suggest, was not furniture for use. It was furniture as an idea. By the mid-1960s, this was an apt metaphor for Danish design more broadly: an idea, originating in Denmark but given form in America.

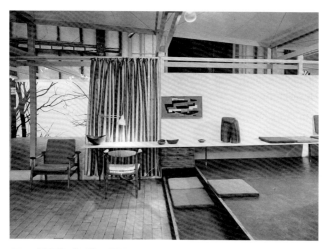

Figure 5.1a *Fremtidens Bolig* (Home of the Future), designed by Finn Juhl, installation view, Cabinetmakers Guild Exhibition, 1954. Landsforeningen Dansk Kunsthaandværk og Kunstindustri, Billedarkiv. DesignMuseum Danmark. Photographer unknown. **Figure 5.1b** *Fremtidens Bolig* (Home of the Future), designed by Finn Juhl, installation view, Cabinetmakers Guild Exhibition, 1954. *Møbler* (1954). Photographer unknown.

Afterword

In 1954, five years after Finn Juhl's Chieftain and Hans Wegner's Round Chair were designed, Juhl paired them in an installation he conceived for that year's Cabinetmakers Exhibition, a jubilee honoring the four hundredth anniversary of the Cabinetmakers Guild. Juhl's *Fremtidens Bolig* (Home of the Future) was a full-scale, furnished house complete with a tiled courtyard and fully grown tree. Such a display would not have fit inside Kunstindustrimuseet, but for the special celebratory exhibition the cabinetmakers had rented out Forum, a large convention center just north of Frederiksberg, where Juhl had been raised. The model house, nearly two thousand square feet, excluding the terrace, was roughly the size of the one he had designed and built for himself a decade prior. Within the structure, Juhl placed three Round Chairs around the dining table, and a fourth in front of a long countertop that could be used as a desk (fig. 5.1a). The Chieftain was lined up behind this fourth Chair, against a wall on the opposite side of the room, as though to allow its sitter to admire the construction of Wegner's design (fig. 5.1b). Juhl's decision to prominently place the two designs across from one another emphasizes the relation between the Chieftain and the Chair and highlights what one curator has recently referred to as "Danish furniture design's breakthrough year, 1949."[1] The home of the future, Juhl seemed to suggest, would be built atop the past.

Juhl's installation was part of a midcentury, international trend in model homes designed to imagine future dwellings. Many, like Frigidaire's Kitchen of Tomorrow (1956), Peter and Alison Smithson's House of the Future (1956), and Monsanto's House of the Future (1957), imagined a future defined by the new—new design ideas like standardization and prefabrication, new technologies like a climate-control panel that dispensed fragrance, new materials like plastic. Juhl's house featured none of these. It was instead part of an alternative strand of futurist visions that, like the fifteen single-family homes in the Town of Tomorrow at the 1939 New York World's Fair and the Case Study Houses sponsored by *Arts & Architecture* magazine (1945–1966), imagined a future already fully realizable in the present. Juhl's Home of the Future included an interior courtyard, a semi-open plan in which sliding doors could be used to close off rooms, existing technology (television, radio) that was already on the rise, and wooden furniture from years past. In addition to the Chieftain and the Chair, the home was dressed in old designs like Kaare Klint's Safari Chair (1933), which was placed in the hallway. Arranged on the steps between the living and dining rooms, cushions from a Torsten Johansson seating range (1953) transformed the passageway into a recreational space. Filled with cabinetmaker-made furniture, *Fremtidens Bolig* was an homage to the past, present, and future of Danish design as conceived by Copenhagen's design community.

While Juhl's primary ambition in designing the house was to test out what he called "experiments" in domestic architecture, with particular attention to devising spaces for work and play, he also described it as an "attempt to show how modern Danish furniture acts in architectural interiors."[2] His interest in how furniture "acts" suggests an underlying belief that furniture is responsive. It behaves differently depending on what is around it, and what is around it can be neither predicted nor fixed. He understood that the concept of a home of the future in which everything was new was unrealistic; rarely was new furniture bought at the same time as, and specifically to suit, a new house.[3] Furniture from different decades would coexist in interiors, and the Chieftain, the Chair, and the other designs he selected would outfit different kinds of spaces. While occasionally the pieces would make their way into entirely modern architectural interiors—Edith Farnsworth's Mies-designed house with its Round Chairs, the Breuer house near Baltimore with its Chieftain—this was the exception rather than the rule. The designs would be used in older houses or paired with a variety of furniture styles old and new. What's more, the environs were sure to change over time and, thus, so would how the furniture behaved. Furniture would outlive the moment of its inception and, in the process, evolve.

As if to insist upon the point, Juhl included in his Home of the Future a wall-mounted sofa with a cantilevered tubular steel frame, which he had previously included in his commission for *Interior-52*, a period room for the then-present day, at the National Museum of Decorative Arts and Design in Trondheim, Norway, where he had placed it alongside a Chieftain Chair. By including the design first in a room typifying an interior of today (circa 1952) and then, two years later, in a house envisioning the home of tomorrow, Juhl acknowledged the rather obvious but easily overlooked fact that furniture has a life beyond the present. The Chieftain, the Chair, and the other pieces that outfitted *Fremtidens Bolig*, Juhl proposed, were furnishing not just for the 1950s but for the decades beyond.

The Chieftain and the Chair seem to acknowledge this endurance and transformation in their very materiality. Whether rendered in teak, oak, walnut, or mahogany, both were only ever finished in natural oil or wax. This surface treatment gave the chairs a tempered, matte look and also affected how their appearance would change over time. Some design writers regard this feature as fundamental to Wegner's furniture, with its "natural finishes" that "not only enhanced the wood's tactile warmth, but in time would darken slightly to form a fine patina."[4] In fact, it is more broadly characteristic, of the Chieftain, too, and of Danish design as a category. "Treated only with oil or wax," explained *arkitekt* Steen Eiler Rasmussen in an English-language article published in a special issue of the *Danish Foreign Office Journal*, "it is left to daylight to give the wood the natural deep brownish tone that never fades but becomes more and more intense."[5] Rasmussen offered his rumination on material as a kind of admiring ode. He was not alone in his opinion; according to a late 1950s poll, most Danes regarded finish as the primary marker of furniture's quality, recognizing natural oil and wax as superior to varnish.[6] Americans also admired the matte finish, "as pleasant to the touch as to the eye," observed one columnist.[7] But if the natural oil or wax finish signaled quality, it also required great care because it made the furniture more susceptible to stains.

Wood will change color not just through exposure to air but also because of what touches it. A tabletop will collect on its surface the rings from sweating cups and glasses and pick up oil from hands and fingers. If an oil or wax finish permits the furniture to develop a rich patina over time, it also allows it to register the marks of use. While some furniture sellers worried that buyers would not understand how to care for their Danish furniture, causing it to stain rather than patina, and some buyers wished that their furniture were not so porous, others romanticized the material's potential for transfiguration.[8] "Wood," wrote Danish critic Knud Poulsen on the occasion of the second-to-last Cabinetmakers Exhibition in 1965, "shall submit itself to the caressing touch, it shal [*sic*] grow under our hands."[9] Echoing Juhl's idea that furniture changes in response to its context of use, Poulsen suggested that, more than other kinds of modern furniture, Danish design, because of its surface treatment, would be transformed by those who encountered it.

Poulsen's poetic reflection on wood offers a cogent metaphor for Danish design more broadly. It grew under the hands of many—designers and makers, retailers and tastemakers, consumers and copyists. Following their initial conception and fabrication, the Chieftain and the Chair were transformed through processes of circulation, use, and reproduction, through the ways they moved in the world after the initial ideas left the designers' drawing studios and the objects themselves left the workshops where they were made. It was these processes, together, that led to their popularity—and that of Danish design more generally—in America.

This transformation continues into the twenty-first century, which has seen a resurgent embrace of Danish design. It is evident in the midcentury originals coveted by collectors and as part of the broader fad for midcentury modern in contemporary domestic design. The Chieftain and the Chair remain compelling protagonists in this story. A company called NyeKoncept sells a chair that mimics the hulking form of the Chieftain and calls it the "Arne," collapsing the look of Juhl's design with the name recognition of his fellow midcentury Danish designer Arne Jacobsen. (NyeKoncept is one of many companies that spells its name with a *k* to appear more Danish, just as Danish companies at midcentury used an *x* to make their furniture seem more international.) And Target sells a "Presidential Dining Armchair" that takes its shape from Wegner's Round Chair, while its name alludes to the Chair's appearance in the Kennedy-Nixon presidential debates. Borrowing their look from Juhl's and Wegner's mid-twentieth-century designs, these twenty-first-century copies also extend and evolve the legacy of Danish design. Danish design did not rise to prominence purely by virtue of its merit, but neither has the more recent fad for it, in which the furniture pieces are billed as timeless. (Such a campaign was already in the works in the 1960s, when Den Permanente began advertising 1950s-era designs by Wegner and others as "*ny klassiker*"—new classics.[10])

Today, the term Danish Modern continues to be thrown around freely on style blogs and Craigslist postings. It has become a catchall for a certain look associated with the midcentury period and defined by wood construction, splayed and swollen legs, and floating forms. Though the story of the Danish Modern revival has yet to be told, the fact of it makes clear that the Chieftain and the Chair continue to grow under our hands.

Acknowledgments

The Chieftain and the Chair were conceived and made by talented men, but this book that bears their names exists because of the smart and intellectually generous women who were my teachers, mentors, and critics during more than ten years of speculating, researching, writing, editing, rewriting, and rewriting again.

Christine Mehring encouraged the project from the start, recognizing a potential that I hope to have approached. From the very beginning she offered mentorship rooted in respect, collegiality, trust, and optimism. Working with her was a gift.

Susan Bielstein, a lion of publishing, was a patient editor who pushed me in all the best ways. I am fortunate for this opportunity to have worked with her a second time.

Aden Kumler's early interest in the project fueled my confidence in it.

Debbie Nelson's reminder that it is easy to criticize existing scholarship but difficult to locate the seeds for new thinking continues to orient my intellectual compass.

A brief conversation with Leora Auslander, in which she asked about the origins of teak, redirected my research in transformative ways.

Anja Lollesgaard and Mirjam Gelfer-Jørgensen welcomed me into the library at DesignMuseum Danmark by sharing resources and afternoon tea. What a true pleasure and privilege to have worked alongside and learned from them.

Over the years, Carma Gorman, Elizabeth Guffey, Robin Landa, and Aaris Sherin have modeled kind and welcoming citizenship in an intellectual community. I aspire to live up to their standard.

Thanks also to Nicolai de Gier and Merete Ahnfeldt-Mollerup at the Royal Academy School of Architecture in Copenhagen; Lars Dybdahl, Nils Frederiksen, Sara Fruelund, Peter Jacobsen, and Christian Holmsted Olesen at DesignMuseum Danmark and its library; the brilliant designer Bodil Kjær; Jørn Guldberg at the University of Southern Denmark; Eeva-Liisa Pelkonen at Yale University; Joseph Loewenstein and Anca Parvulescu at Washington University in St. Louis; the Greenberg/Freilich family; Toby Wu, Shane Rothe, and Daniel H. Walden; Dylan Montanari, Carrie Adams, and the incomparable Joel Score at the University of Chicago Press, and the three anonymous readers invited by the Press; and friends and fellow thinkers Hadji Bakara, Venus Bivar, Annie Bostrom, Ellen Chu, Alexandra Fraser, Kathryn Hardy, Mia Khimm, Jessica Paga, Samantha Seeley, Jenn Sichel, and Anca Stoica.

This book was made possible by generous grants and fellowships from the Doolittle-Harrison Travel Fellowship, the Smart Family Foundation Fellowship, and the Kathleen Shelton Memorial Travel Fellowship (all at the University of Chicago), the Fulbright Program, the Center for Advanced Study in the Visual Arts, the American-Scandinavian Foundation, the Lois Roth Foundation, the American Council of Learned Societies, the Graham Foundation for Advanced Study in the Fine Arts , and the Neil Harris Endowment Fund at the University of Chicago Press.

My deepest thanks are reserved for those I love dearly: my dad, Ron, who was my first writing teacher, my best writing teacher, and my writing teacher still; my mom, Molli, who has always modeled a love for reading, and whose company and care sustain me; Jamie, my sister in spirit, whose support is unwavering; Alex—my partner in traipsing, catch, bike rides, donut days, the spelling bee, the stuff of life—whose interest and curiosity inspires mine; and our sons, Abe, for whom the question "Why?" is a constant refrain, and Emil, whose pending arrival forced me to finally (finally!) finish this decade-plus project.

Now that it is done, I carry forward the image of Abe sitting on Wegner's Round Chair, dressed in striped pajamas, legs splayed, hair wet from the bath, blowing on a whistle, resisting bedtime, filling our home with the sounds, satisfactions, laughter, frustrations, silliness, and joys of love.

Notes

References to the archives of DesignMuseum Danmark, Copenhagen, are abbreviated "DMD," followed by collection number and last name of the subjects listed here: Arkiv 14 (Poul Christiansen, Snedkermesterlaugets Udstillinger); Arkiv 119 (Asger Fischer); Arkiv 120 (Finn Juhl).

Introduction

1   George Tanier, quoted in William L. Hamilton, "Design Notebook; What's Cool, Calm and Collected? Nordic Modern," *New York Times*, February 26, 1998, http://www.nytimes.com/1998/02/26/garden/design-notebook-what-s-cool-calm-and-collected-nordic-modern.html.

2   Elaine Louie, "Danish Modern Is Hot," *New York Times*, October 6, 1994, https://www.nytimes.com/1994/10/06/garden/danish-modern-is-hot.html.

3   *Mobilia* 21, no. 7 (July 1955): n.p.

4   Joan Kron, "Home Beat," *New York Times*, December 1, 1977, DMD Arkiv 120 (Juhl).

5   Mary Roche, "The Growing Love of Soft, Rounded Flowing Forms," *House Beautiful*, October 1952, 184–85.

6   "Danske Møbler til U.S.A.," *Mobilia* 2, no. 2 (February 1956): 23.

7   *Historical Statistics of the United States, Colonial Times to 1970* (Washington, DC: US Department of Commerce, Bureau of the Census, 1975), 844; "Danske Møbler til U.S.A.," *Mobilia* 22, no. 2 (February 1956): 24, 26.

8   "A. J. Iversen: Diverse artikler om Snedkerlaugets Møbeludstillinger," DMD Arkiv 14 (Christiansen).

9   See, for example, Kevin Davies, "Markets, Marketing and Design: The Danish Furniture Industry c. 1947–65," *Scandinavian Journal of Design History* 9 (1999): 56–73; Per H. Hansen, "Networks, Narratives, and New Markets: The Rise and Decline of Danish Modern Furniture Design, 1930–1970," *Business History Review* 80 (Autumn 2006): 449–83; Per H. Hansen, *Danish Modern Furniture, 1930–2016: The Rise, Decline and Re-emergence of a Cultural Market Category*, trans. Mark Mussari (Odense: University Press of Southern Denmark, 2018).

10 *Historical Statistics of the United States*, 639.

11   Elaine Tyler May, *Homeward Bound: American Families in the Cold War Era* (New York: Basic Books, 1988), 165.

12   Monica Obniski, "Selling the Scandinavian Dream," in *Scandinavian Design and the United States 1890–1980*, ed. Bobbye Tigerman and Monica Obniski (New York: Prestel, 2020), 72.

13   *Design in Scandinavia*, exh. cat., ed. Arne Remlov (Oslo: Kirstes Boktrykkeri, 1954), 11; Edgar Kaufmann Jr., "Scandinavian Design in the U.S.A.," *Interiors*, May 1954, 108.

14   Eeva-Liisa Pelkonen uses the figure of Alvar Aalto to address the case of Finland in *Alvar Aalto: Architecture, Modernity, and Geopolitics* (New Haven, CT: Yale University Press, 2009). Kjetil Fallan has told Norway's specific story in *Designing Modern Norway: A History of Design Discourse* (London: Routledge, 2016).

15   Kron, "Home Beat," DMD Arkiv 120 (Juhl).

16   Kron, "Home Beat," DMD Arkiv 120 (Juhl).

17   Elizabeth Gordon, "Why the New Scandinavian Show Is Important to America," *House Beautiful*, February 1954, 94; Elizabeth Gordon, "Does Design Have Social Significance?" *House Beautiful*, October 1953, 313.

Chapter One

1   "Rundt om Finn Juhl—et interview," *Rum og Form* 4, no. 81 (April 6, 1982): 7.

2   Finn Juhl, "Some Notes on Design," DMD Arkiv 120 (Juhl).

3   Margarete Berger, "Danska Möbelsnickare," *Sydsvenska Dagbladet Snällposten*, October 4, 1947.

4   See, for example, Christian Bundegaard, *Finn Juhl: Life, Work, World* (London: Phaidon, 2019), 15.

5   "Center of Modern Design: Illums Bolighus" (pamphlet) (Copenhagen: Illums Bolighus, May 1959), DesignMuseum Denmark, Copenhagen.

6   Birte [Birte Strangaard], "Møbler med et dobbeltliv," *Aftenbladet*, September 30, 1949.

7   *Rum og Form* 4, no. 81 (April 6, 1982): 7.

8   Advertisement, *Amager Bladet*, December 7, 1942.

9   Scrapbook, vol. 2, Fritz Hansen Archives, Fritz Hansen A/S, Lillerød, Denmark.

10   Knud J. V. Jespersen, *A History of Denmark* (Basingstoke, UK: Palgrave Macmillan, 2004), 177.

11   Mary-Louise Larsen, "Danish Modern: A Good King, and Socialism That Doesn't Show . . . ," *Vogue* 106, no. 11 (December 15, 1945): 106.

12 "De københavnske boligtypers udvikling" (The Development of Copenhagen Housing Types), *Arkitekten* 38, no. 5 (1936); "Københavnske boligtyper fra 1914 til 1936" (Copenhagen Housing Types from 1914 to 1936), *Arkitekten* 38, nos. 6–7 (1936).

13 i., "Fra den 2 Værelses til Kongens Bibliotek," *Horsens Folkeblad*, October 23, 1953; kit. (Aase Wessel Gliemann), "Hvordan bør vi indrette os?" *Jyllands-Posten* (Aarhus), October 3, 1955. That some of these compact designs, like Hans Olsen's settee sleeper, were exported to the US in large numbers suggests it was not only for Copenhageners that they were conceived.

14 *Møbleringsplaner ved Byggebogen* (Copenhagen: I Kommission hos Teknisk Forlag, 1958).

15 Børge Glahn, in *Arkitekten* (1949), quoted in Grete Jalk, ed., *40 Years of Danish Furniture Design* (Copenhagen: Lindhardt and Ringhof, 2017), 3:98.

16 Hans Wegner, quoted in Christian Holmsted Olesen, *Wegner: Just One Good Chair*, trans. Mark Mussari (Ostfildern: Hatje Cantz, 2014), 131.

17 Marianne Wegner, email to the author, April 5, 2022.

18 Ole Wanscher, in *Arkitekten* (1935), quoted in Jalk, *40 Years of Danish Furniture Design*, 1:204.

19 Hans Wegner, quoted in Olesen, *Wegner*, 131.

20 A decade after Wegner designed the Chair, on the occasion of a solo exhibition at the Georg Jensen shop in New York, an American magazine would write, "The inspiration for it was a Chinese child's chair in a Copenhagen museum." "Hans Wegner's One-Man Show at Georg Jensen," *Interiors*, February 1959, 83.

21 Kaare Klint, "Undervisningen i møbeltegning ved Kunstakademier," *Arkitekten* 13, no. 10 (October 1930): 200.

22 Steen Eiler Rasmussen, "Modern Danish Design," *Journal of the Royal Society of Arts* 96, no. 4761 (January 30, 1948).

23 Hakon Stephensen, in *Politiken*, quoted in Jalk, *40 Years of Danish Furniture Design*, 1:28.

24 *Udstilling af Møbelhaandværk arrangeret af Københavns Snedkerlaugs* (1927), DMD Arkiv 14 (Christiansen).

25 *Udstilling af Møbelhaandværk arrangeret af Københavns Snedkerlaugs* (1930), DMD Arkiv 14 (Christiansen).

26 Bent Salicath, "A Survey of Modern Danish Industrial Design" (unpublished manuscript, ca. 1963), DMD Arkiv 119 (Fischer).

27 P. U. V. to Snedkerlaugets Møbeludstillinger (letter, June 1958), DMD Arkiv 14 (Christiansen).

28 Nils Borén, chairman's report, March 8, 1934, quoted in Per H. Hansen, *Danish Modern Furniture, 1930–2016: The Rise, Decline and Re-emergence of a Cultural Market Category*, trans. Mark Mussari (Odense: University Press of Southern Denmark, 2018), 107.

29 A. J. Iversen to H. Jerichow (letter, February 13, 1959), DMD Arkiv 14 (Christiansen).

30 *Snedkermesterlauget's Udstilling på Charlottenborg 1938* (film), DesignMuseum Danmark, Copenhagen.

31 A. J. Iversen to H. Jerichow (letter, February 13, 1959); "Ministeriet for Handel, Håndværk, Industri og Søfart, Slotsholmsgade 10, København K., 24 October 1957"—both DMD Arkiv 14 (Christiansen).

32 See, for example, Fridelin, "Stole som sivbaljer og svævende sofaer," *Social-Demokraten*, September 22, 1950; Steph (Hakon Stephensen), "De fineste møbler faar man i Danmark," *Politiken*, September 22, 1950.

33 Willy Hansen, in *N.T.K.*, quoted in Jalk, *40 Years of Danish Furniture Design*, 1:88.

34 Betty Pepis, "For the Home: Danish Craft Designs Stem from the Traditional," *New York Times*, July 15, 1950, 16.

35 Poul Christiansen, "Snedkerlaugets Møbeludstillinger" (1957), DMD Arkiv 14 (Christiansen).

36 *Snedkerlaugets Udstilling 1927* (brochure), DesignMuseum Danmark, Copenhagen.

37 "Snedkerlaugets Udstilling 1950," DMD Arkiv 14 (Christiansen).

38 "Snedkerne staar for skud," *Berlingske Aftenavis*, October 1, 1958.

39 D. A., "Danish Furniture: Old Hands Give Shape to New Ideas," *Interiors*, February 1950, 87.

40 D. A., "Danish Furniture: Old Hands Give Shape to New Ideas," *Interiors*, February 1950, 90, 89

41 Finn Juhl, "Finn Juhl," *Nordenfjeldske Kunstindustrimuseum Årbok 1950* (Trondheim: Nordenfjeldske Kunstindustrimuseum, 1950), 24.

42 Henrik Sten Møller, "Finn Juhl and His Gentleman's House and Furniture" (pamphlet) (GEC Gads Forlag, 1990), 2.

Chapter Two

1 K. H.—ck., "Möbelevenemang i Köpenhamn," *Svenska Dagbladet*, October 6, 1949.

2 Jota, "Danska experimentmöbler väcker svenskt intresse," *Dagens Nyheter*, October 21, 1949.

3 flm. (Flemming Madsen), "Danske Møbler faar blaat Stempel i USA," *Berlingske*

Aftenavis, September 24, 1949; Birte (Birte Strandgaard), "Mere om møbler," *Aften-bladet*, October 1, 1949.

4   Birte (Birte Strandgaard), "Mere om møbler," *Aftenbladet*, October 1, 1949.

5   Brooklyn Museum Archives, Records of the Department of Public Information, "Press releases, 1916–1930," 1927, 074–82.

6   Edgar Kaufmann Jr., "Finn Juhl of Copenhagen," *Interiors*, November 1948, 96.

7   Sven Markelius, a Swede, and Arnstein Arneberg, a Norwegian, were commissioned to design the other two primary assembly halls—the Economic and Social Council chamber and the Security Council chamber, respectively.

8   Kaufmann chaired the 1951 selection committee, whose members were William Friedman, assistant director of the Walker Art Center in Minneapolis; Philip Johnson, MoMA's director of Architecture and Design; Hugh Lawson, divisional merchandise manager for the Chicago department store Carson Pirie Scott & Co.; and architect Eero Saarinen.

9   "Finn Juhl" (market report), June 1956, Baker Furniture Company Collection, Grand Rapids Public Library, Grand Rapids, MI.

10 "Baker Modern Furniture by Finn Juhl Is Introduced in Dramatic Showing," *Baker Bugle* 8, no. 1 (June 1951): 1; "Baker Introduces a New Modern" (pamphlet; Whitney Publications, 1951), n.p.; "New Modern Group Sets Record for Furniture Designed, Delivered, via Air," *Baker Bugle* 8, no. 1 (June 1951): 1.

11 "Baker Introduces a New Modern."

12 Herman Miller, "America Meets Charles and Ray Eames," YouTube (video, 11:28), 1956, https://www.youtube.com/watch?v=IBLMoMhlAfM.

13 There were other structural differences. For example, five machine-stamped stainless steel tabs, which Baker used on all its Juhl-designed chairs, held the seat in place. And the skeletons for the armrests were made of cast aluminum rather than the planished or cast steel Vodder used. "Baker Furniture," accessed May 28, 2021, https://www.thechieftainchair.com/baker-furniture.

14 "Baker Showing at This Market Emphasizes New Idea of 'One World,'" *Baker Bugle* 14, no. 2 (June 1956): 1.

15 Olga Gueft, "About the Quiet Life of a Danish Architect," *Interiors*, September 1950, 85. Quoted in *Baker Bugle* 7, no. 1 (January 1951): 3.

16 "Danish Furniture," *Mobilia* 22, no. 7 (July 1956): 4, 5.

17 Christian Holmsted Olesen, *Wegner: Just One Good Chair*, trans. Mark Mussari (Ostfildern: Hatje Cantz, 2014), 62.

18 "Export Furniture", *Mobilia* 22, no. 2 (February 1956): 34–37. According to economic

historian Per H. Hansen, Johannes Hansen initially turned down the order before ultimately filling it. The cabinetmaker claimed to occasionally receive and fill large orders
for a hundred or more of Wegner's Round Chair. Hansen, *Danish Modern Furniture,
1930–2016: The Rise, Decline and Reemergence of a Cultural Market Category*, trans.
Mark Mussari (Odense: University Press of Southern Denmark, 2018), 334.

19 Asger Fischer to Udenrigsministeriet (letter, April 9, 1946), Den Permanente Collection, Erhvervsarkivet, Aarhus, DK.

20 "Amerikanske importører om skandinaviske møbler," *Mobilia* 21, no. 8 (August 1955): n.p.

21 Ejnar Pedersen, quoted in Samuel Rachlin, *Håndværk og Livsvaerk: Ejnar Pedersen,
snedker* (Copenhagen: Gyldendal, 2014), translated and reprinted in "Niels Vodder,"
accessed July 21, 2020, https://www.thechieftainchair.com/niels-vodder.

22 Ulf Hård af Segerstad, *Modern Scandinavian Furniture* (Totowa, NJ: Bedminster Press,
1963), 32, 35; Esbjørn Hiort, "Trends in Contemporary Danish Design," in *The Arts of
Denmark: Viking to Modern*, exh. cat. (New York: Metropolitan Museum of Art; Landsforeningen Dansk Kunsthaandværk, 1960), 122–24.

23 Hansen, *Danish Modern Furniture*, 325.

24 "En haandsnedker bruger da maskiner," *Politiken*, February 20, 1955.

25 Niels Vodder, "Finn Juhl Møbler" (pamphlet), 1956, DesignMuseum Danmark, Copenhagen.

26 *Good Design* master checklist, n.p., accessed April 3, 2022, https://assets.moma.org/
documents/moma_master-checklist_325812.pdf?_ga=2.228837082.754922418.164903
3740-122288114.1648780134.

27 "Et diskret akkompagnement . . . : Snedkermester Johs. Hansens nye forretningsloka-
ler indrettet af Hans J. Wegner," *Møbler* 30, no. 9 (September 1953): 28.

28 David Greenberg and Marian Greenberg, *The Shopping Guide to Europe* (New York:
Harper & Bros., 1954), 215.

29 Kirsten Jennen (letter, September 1, 1955), "Placitas Chair," accessed April 3, 2022,
https://www.thechieftainchair.com/placitas-chair.

30 James France, *France & Søn: British Pioneers of Danish Furniture* (Copenhagen: For-
laget VITA, 2016), 28.

31 Irv. (Aage Schultz), "Danske Møbler af en helt ny Type fremstillet til Eksport," *Berlingske Tidende*, June 26, 1945.

32 Peniila Laviolette, email to the author, September 10, 2013.

33 "Export Organisation," *Mobilia* 21, no. 11 (November 1955): 57.

34 K. Packness, "Danish Arts and Crafts and the USA," *Dansk Kunsthaandværk*, vol. 24
(1951), quoted in Kevin Davies, "Markets, Marketing and Design: The Danish Furniture

Industry c. 1947–65," *Scandinavian Journal of Design History* 9 (1999): 62n17.

35   *Dansk Arbejde* (November 1951), quoted in Davies, "Markets, Marketing and Design," 62.

36   *Social-Demokraten*, June 6, 1954, cited in Widar Halén, "The Flow of Ideas USA–Scandinavia," in *Scandinavian Design beyond the Myth: Fifty Years of Scandinavian Design from the Nordic Countries*, ed. Widar Halén and Kerstin Wickman (Stockholm: Arvinius Förlag/Form Förlag, 2003), 54n28.

37   Halén, "Flow of Ideas USA–Scandinavia," 54.

38   ulla, "Lette smukke møbler på årets møbeludstilling," *Land og Folk*, September 18, 1959.

39   "Un-Matched Beauty: Pink and Red," *Vogue* 117, no. 9 (May 15, 1951): 49.

40   Fandango (Fritze Schlegel), in *Berlingske Tidende*, quoted in Grete Jalk, *40 Years of Danish Furniture Design* (Copenhagen: Teknologisk Instituts Forlag, 2017), 3:164.

41   "Vogue's Early Report," *Vogue* 124, no. 1 (July 1, 1954): C2b.

42   Bent Salicath, "On the Development of Danish Furnishing Textiles," *Contemporary Danish Design in Textiles and Furniture* (San Francisco: De Young Museum, 1957), n.p.

43   Greenberg and Greenberg, *Shopping Guide to Europe*, 216.

44   Greenberg and Greenberg, *Shopping Guide to Europe*, 214.

45   A. V. Jacobsen to Asger Fischer (letter, August 5, 1946), DMD Arkiv 119 (Fischer).

46   Goran F. Holmquist to Asger Fischer (letter, September 9, 1960), DMD Arkiv 119 (Fischer).

47   "Snedkerlaugets 38. Møbeludstilling, Furniture Exhibition, Exhibition de Meubles, Möbelausstelling, 30.10–15.11.1964" (exhibition pamphlet), DMD Arkiv 14 (Christiansen).

48   Viggo Sten Møller, *Dansk Møbel Kunst: Københavns Snedkerlaugs Møbeludstilling* (Copenhagen: Rasmus Navers Forlag, 1951), 30.

49   Frank., "Møblerne bliver dyrere," *B.T.*, September 25, 1947. See also cat. (Carla Højfeldt), "Snedkernes Møbelparade i Kunstindustrimuseet," *Kristeligt Dagblad*, September 26, 1947.

50   Vibeke Sørensen, "The Politic of Closed Markets: Denmark, the Marshall Plan, and European Integration, 1945–1963," *International History Review* 15, no. 1 (February 1993): 29.

51   Boe., "Kongens yndlings-stol er lavet af Århus-arkitekt," *Demokraten*, September 22, 1957.

52   France, *France & Søn*, 66–67.

53   *Danish Foreign Office Journal*, no. 35 (1960).

54   "Stilfærdigt og smukt," *Information*, September 16, 1960; Svend Erik Møller, "Så er det sket med teak-træet," *Politiken*, September 16, 1960; "Dansk møbelarkitektur er stadig paa toppen," *Børsen*, September 16, 1960; Hartung-Nielsen, "Farvel og Tak Teak,"

B.T., September 16, 1960; Ekstramanden, "Et dødsfald," *Ekstrabladet*, September 17, 1960.

55   "Teak ikke færdig paa møbelmarkedet," *Dagens Nyheder (K)*, October 3, 1960.

56   Øjet, "Vi kan stadig lave møbler," *Ekstrabladet*, September 18, 1959.

57   Suchin Worawongwasu, "A Study of Thailand's Balance of Trade 1953–1962," MS thesis, Utah State University, 1964, 53.

58   Sarah Booth Conroy, "The Teak Turnoff," *Washington Post*, October 8, 1978 (emphasis mine).

59   Anne Douglas, "Danish Furniture Tailored to American Market: Both Countries' Skills Reflected in Designs," *Chicago Tribune*, October 13, 1957.

60   A period article reported that Baker Furniture Company funded all of the installation's Juhl-designed furniture and also made the sofa. O.G., "For Tomorrow's Antiquarian," *Interiors*, February 1953, 75.

61   "Modern Furniture by Finn Juhl Exhibited in Europe," *Baker Bugle* 8, no. 1 (June 1951): 3.

Chapter Three

1   Doris H. Scherbak to Asger Fischer (letter, April 18, 1954), DMD Arkiv 119 (Fischer).

2   Doris H. Scherbak to Asger Fischer (letter, July 23, 1953), DMD Arkiv 119 (Fischer).

3   Scherbak to Fischer (letter, April 18, 1954), DMD Arkiv 119 (Fischer).

4   Scherbak to Fischer (letter, April 18, 1954), DMD Arkiv 119 (Fischer).

5   DMD Arkiv 119 (Fischer).

6   "How to Bring Home Your Scandinavian Purchases," *House Beautiful*, July 1959, 121.

7   Den Permanente Collection, Erhvervsarkivet, Aarhus, DK.

8   Helen Robertson to Asger Fischer (letter, May 28, 1954); Marian Manners to Asger Fischer (letter, August 17, 1954); Will Melhorn to Asger Fischer (letter, November 7, 1955); Harold T. Christie to Asger Fischer (letter, August 9, 1955)—all DMD Arkiv 119 (Fischer).

9   National Retail Furniture Association to Asger Fischer (letter, August 15, 1958); John B. Ward to Asger Fischer (letter, January 18, 1950); Aileen Vanderbilt Webb to Asger Fischer (letter, May 10, 1957)—all DMD Arkiv 119 (Fischer).

10   Sigurd Schultz, "Inspiration of Danish Applied Art," *Danish Foreign Office Journal: Commercial and General Review* 132 (January 1932): 3, quoted in Jean Givens, "Craft, Commerce and Den Permanente," *Design and Culture* 7, no. 3, "The Influence of Scandinavian Design" (2015): 339.

11   Asger Fischer, Comments to the National Retail Furniture Association, n.d. (in response to a letter of August 1958), DMD Arkiv 119 (Fischer).

12   *Modern Danish Industrial Art: New York, 1939* (Copenhagen: Forening for Kunsthaand-værk, Den Permanente . . . , 1939), 3–4, 5.

13   *Modern Danish Industrial Art*, 5.

14   "Danish Crafts Film Subjects," *Ottawa Citizen*, November 10, 1949; "What People Are Doing: Women's Film Night at Y.M.C.A," *Canberra Times*, July 13, 1954; "Beta Sigma Phi," *Tri-City Herald*, February 16, 1964.

15   *Shaped by Danish Hands*, Minerva Film (1947), accessed July 14, 2020, https://filmcentralen.dk/museum/danmark-paa-film/film/shaped-danish-hands.

16   *Shaped by Danish Hands*.

17   Børge Jensen, "Snedkerlaugets Møbeludstilling 1963," DMD Arkiv 14 (Christiansen).

18   Naboth Hedin and Folke Bernadotte, "Sweden at the New York World's Fair" (New York: Royal Swedish Commission, New York World's Fair, 1939), n.p.

19   Stops included Brooklyn, Chicago, and Los Angeles. "Nordic Udstilling i U.S.A. 1953," DMD Arkiv 120 (Juhl).

20   Gotthard Johansson, "Design in Scandinavia," in *Design in Scandinavia*, exh. cat., ed. Arne Remlov (Oslo: Kirstes Boktrykkeri, 1954), 20, 12. For more on the development of regional design identity, see Mirjam Gelfer-Jørgensen, "Scandinavianism—a Cultural Brand," in *Scandinavian Design beyond the Myth: Fifty Years of Scandinavian Design from the Nordic Countries*, ed. Widar Halén and Kerstin Wickman (Stockholm: Arvinius Forlag/Form Förlag, 2003), 17.

21   Johansson, "Design in Scandinavia," 12.

22   Finn Juhl, quoted in "Danish Design—Danish Nature," *Mobilia*, n.s., no. 32 (March 1958), n.p.

23   A website run by Jason Kinsella, thechieftainchair.com, details many of these variations and describes the construction particulars of a few especially noteworthy Chieftains.

24   Esbjørn Hiort, "Trends in Contemporary Danish Design," in *The Arts of Denmark: Viking to Modern*, exh. cat. (New York: Metropolitan Museum of Art; Landsforeningen Dansk Kunsthaandværk, 1960), 122.

25   Betty Pepis, "For the Home: Danish Craft Designs Stem-From the Traditional," *New York Times*, July 15, 1950, 16.

26   B. D., "Hans Wegner: The Heresies of a Quiet Dane," *Industrial Design* 6, No. 3 (March 1959), 56.

27   Marilyn Hoffman, "Design in Scandinavia," *Christian Science Monitor*, July 9, 1954.

28   Edgar Kaufmann Jr., "Finn Juhl on the American Scene" (unpublished manuscript for a lecture at Columbia University, New York, ca. 1956), DMD Arkiv 120 (Juhl).

29   Kaufmann, "Finn Juhl on the American Scene," DMD Arkiv 120 (Juhl).

30   D. A., "Danish Furniture: Old Hands Give Shape to New Ideas," *Interiors*, February 1950, 90, 89.

31   Eliot Noyes, *Organic Design in Home Furnishings* (New York: Museum of Modern Art, 1941).

32   Edgar Kaufmann Jr., "An American View of the Arts of Denmark and Danish Modern Design," in *Arts of Denmark*, 99, 103.

33   Kaufmann, "American View," 106.

34   Christopher Tunnard and Henry Hope Reed, *American Skylines: The Growth and Form of Our Cities and Towns* (New York: New American Library, 1956), 73–74.

35   Grete Jalk, "Shaker Furniture," *Mobilia*, n.s., no. 138 (January 1967).

36   Leslie Cheek Jr., "Do Americans Have Good Taste," *New York Times*, June 6, 1954.

37   Draft of a letter to the Swedish Ministry of Trade, July 8, 1938, Archive of the Swedish Institute in the National Archives, quoted in Kerstin Wickman, "Design Olympics—the Milan Triennials," in Halén and Wickman, *Scandinavian Design beyond the Myth*, 38.

38   Gotthard Johansson, "Design in Scandinavia," in *Design in Scandinavia* (Oslo: Kirstes Boktrykkeri, 1954), 12.

39   Elizabeth Gordon, "Why the New Scandinavian Show Is Important to America," *House Beautiful*, February 1954, 14.

40   "Emigrants' Loyalties Described," *Washington Post*, October 18, 1925, E15; Madison Grant, "The Racial Transformation of America," *North American Review* 219, no. 820 (March 1924): 349. Both quoted in Erin Leary, "'The Total Absence of Foreign Subjects': The Racial Politics of US Interwar Exhibitions of Scandinavian Design," *Design and Culture* 7, no. 3, "The Influence of Scandinavian Design" (November 2015): 293.

41   Reyner Banham, "Is There a Substitute for Wood Grain Plastic?," in *Design and Aesthetics in Wood*, ed. Eric A. Anderson and George F. Earle (New York: SUNY College of Environmental Science and Forestry, 1972), 9, 10.

42   Elizabeth Gordon, "The Beauty That Comes with Common Sense," *House Beautiful*, July 1959, 57, 56.

43   Gordon, "Beauty That Comes with Common Sense," 57, 56.

44   Elizabeth Gordon, "The Threat to the Next America," *House Beautiful*, April 1953, 129, 127.

45   Gordon, "Why the New Scandinavian Show Is Important," 14.

46   "Udkast til formandens beretning for 1959," Thorald Madsen Archive, Erhvervsarkivet, Aarhus, Denmark. Quoted in Per H. Hansen, *Danish Modern Furniture, 1930–2016: The*

Rise, Decline and Re-emergence of a Cultural Market Category, trans. Mark Mussari (Odense: University Press of Southern Denmark, 2018), 288.

47 Fischer, Comments to the National Retail Furniture Association, DMD Arkiv 119 (Fischer).

48 Gordon, "Beauty That Comes with Common Sense," 56–57.

49 Marion Gough, "Hans J. Wegner: Poet of Practicality," *House Beautiful*, July 1959, 114 (also 65).

50 Gough, "Hans J. Wegner," 65.

51 Marion Gough, "If Your Home Is Your Hobby . . . Take a Trip to Scandinavia," *House Beautiful*, February 1951, 102–4, 106, 108, 110, 113–14, 116–18, 124–26, 145–46.

52 Gough, "Hans J. Wegner," 66.

53 See, for example, "Lille snak om fynboer og hest," *Tidens Kvinder*, no. 29 (July 19, 1955), 26–27.

54 Janet Callahan, "Denmark Delights US Shoppers," *Cincinnati Post*, January 4, 1950.

55 Finn Juhl, quoted in Torsten Boheman, "Arkitekter og Møbler," *Møbelhandleren*, June 1951, 22.

56 Doris H. Scherbak to Asger Fischer (letter, December 14, 1954), DMD Arkiv 119 (Fischer).

57 Doris H. Scherbak to Asger Fischer (letter, May 21, 1954), DMD Arkiv 119 (Fischer).

58 Doris H. Scherbak to Asger Fischer (letter, July 12, 1956), DMD Arkiv 119 (Fischer).

59 Rosalie S. Fasolu to Asger Fischer (letter, May 17, 1952), DMD Arkiv 119 (Fischer).

60 Cyra Sanborn to Asger Fischer (letter, January 31, 1957), DMD Arkiv 119 (Fischer).

61 David Greenberg to Asger Fischer (letter, October 19, 1953), DMV Arkiv 119 (Fischer).

62 Asger Fischer to Elizabeth Gordon (letter, April 17, 1957), DMD Arkiv 119 (Fischer).

63 A. R. J. Friedmann to Asger Fischer (letter, August 23, 1957), DMV Arkiv 119 (Fischer) Proforma Invoice, Den Permanente, "Placitas Chair," accessed June 21, 2021, https://www.thechieftainchair.com/placitas-chair.

64 Harold H. Burton to Asger Fischer (letter, December 21, 1953), DMD Arkiv 119 (Fischer).

65 David Greenberg to Asger Fischer (letter, May 26, 1954), DMD Arkiv 119 (Fischer).

66 David Greenberg and Marian Greenberg, *The Shopping Guide to Europe* (New York: Harper and Bros., 1954). O'Toole's annotated copy is in the author's collection.

67 Greenberg and Greenberg, *Shopping Guide to Europe*, 215.

68 Greenberg and Greenberg, *Shopping Guide to Europe*, 216.

69 David Greenberg to Asger Fischer (letter, November 19, 1953), DMD Arkiv 119 (Fischer).

70 Rose van Sand to Asger Fischer (letter, September 9, 1948), DMD Arkiv 119: Asger (Fischer).

Chapter Four

1   Lis Laugesen (letter, June 28, 1957), "Placitas Chair," accessed June 23, 2021, https://www.thechieftainchair.com/placitas-chair.

2   Marion Gough, "Hans J. Wegner: Poet of Practicality," *House Beautiful*, July 1959, 65.

3   Doris H. Scherbak to Asger Fischer (letter, July 12, 1956), DMD Arkiv 119 (Fischer).

4   David Greenberg and Marian Greenberg, *The Shopping Guide to Mexico, Guatemala, and the Carribbean, also Bermuda, Nassau, and Panama* (New York: Trade Winds Press, 1955), 36.

5   "Designed and Made in the U.S.A.," *House Beautiful*, July 1959, 89.

6   Quoted in "Danish Design—Danish Nature," *Mobilia*, n.s., no. 32 (March 1958), n.p.

7   Gough, "Hans J. Wegner," 66.

8   Carma Gorman, "Law as a Lens for Understanding Design," *Design and Culture* 6, no. 3, "Design and the Law" (November 2014): 269–90.

9   Gorman, "Law as a Lens," 277.

10 Gorman, "Law as a Lens," 278.

11 Carma Gorman, "How U.S. Law Shapes American Design: The Evolution of IP Design Protection," *Texas CEO Magazine*, August 8, 2015, https://texasceomagazine.com/how-u-s-law-shapes-american-design/.

12 Gorman, "How U.S. Law Shapes American Design."

13 Anne Neglia, quoted in D., "Plagiaterne endnu engang . . . ," *Møbler* 31, no. 4 (April 1954), 38–39.

14 Joan Kron, "Home Beat," *New York Times*, December 1, 1977, DMD Arkiv 120 (Juhl).

15 Edgar Kaufmann Jr., "Finn Juhl on the American Scene" (unpublished manuscript for a lecture at Columbia University, New York, ca. 1956), DMD Arkiv 120 (Juhl).

16 Kron, "Home Beat," DMD Arkiv 120 (Juhl).

17 Hans Wegner, quoted in Betsy Darrachi, "Hans Wegner's One-Man Show at Georg Jensen," *Interiors*, February 1959, 84.

18 D., "Plagiaterne endnu engang . . . ," 39.

19 Gunnar Iversen, "Eksport af danske møbler," *Snedkermestrenes Medlemsblad* 50, no. 1 (January 1949), 5.

20 Zenith ad, *Reader's Digest* (special detachable section), 1966; Magnavox Debs Concert Grand Stereo Console advertisement, *Billboard*, ca. 1959.

21 Margarete Berger, "Danska Möbelsnickare," *Sydsvenska Dagbladet Snällposten*, October 4, 1947.

22 Kristina Wilson, *Mid-Century Modernism and the American Body: Race, Gender, and*

the Politics of Power in Design (Princeton, NJ: Princeton University Press, 2021), 100–104, 186–88.

23 Jeffrey Meikle, *Twentieth Century Limited: Industrial Design in America 1925–1939* (Philadelphia, PA: Temple University Press, 1979), 181; Carma Gorman, "Educating the Eye: Body Mechanics and Streamlining in the United States, 1925–1950," *American Quarterly* 58, no. 3, "'Rewiring the 'Nation': The Place of Technology in American Studies" (September 2006): 839–68.

24 Gorman, "Educating the Eye," 861, 863.

25 See, for example, Margaret Sanger, "The Need of Birth Control in America," in Adolf Meyer, ed. *Birth Control: Facts and Responsibilities* (Baltimore: Williams and Wilkins Co., 1925), 15, quoted in Christina Cogdell, "The Futurama Recontextualized: Norman Bel Geddes's Eugenic 'World of Tomorrow,'" *American Quarterly* 52, no. 2 (June 2000): 200.

26 Architectural historian Dianne Harris has observed that in the 1940s and 1950s, "dirt, crowding, trash, lack of privacy, and untidy spaces signaled poverty and insecure racial identities. In contrast, clutter-free and clean environments were construed as belonging to middle-class, white occupants." Harris, *Little White Houses* (Minneapolis: University of Minnesota Press, 2013), 98.

27 Gough, "Hans J. Wegner," 65.

28 *Vore dages møbler. Et håndvaerks vej i en maskintid* (Copenhagen: Johannes Hansen, 1954).

29 "Danish Furniture Knocks Down for Moving," *Popular Science* (February 1947), 169; *Speculum* (College of Veterinary Medicine, Ohio State University), 14–15 (1960): 39.

30 Lis Laugesen (letter, June 28, 1957), "Placitas Chair," accessed June 23, 2021, https://www.thechieftainchair.com/placitas-chair.

31 *Sears Christmas 1962*, Sears, Roebuck and Co., Chicago, Illinois, 201; "Marketing for America for More than a Hundred Years, Sears Catalogs Have Been a Supply Tool and a Barometer of Daily Life in the Heartland," *South Florida Sun Sentinel*, November 4, 1987, https://www.sun-sentinel.com/news/fl-xpm-1987-11-04-8702030605-story.html.

32 Willy Hansen, *Nyt Tidsskrift for Kunstindustri*, 88, quoted in Grete Jalk, *40 Years of Danish Furniture Design* (Copenhagen: Teknologisk Instituts Forlag, 2017), 1:88.

33 Tell City Chair Company brochure, quoted in Per H. Hansen, "Networks, Narratives, and New Markets: The Rise and Decline of Danish Modern Furniture Design, 1930–1970," *Business History Review* 80 (Autumn 2006): 460.

34 Poul Christiansen, "Åbningen af Snedkerlaugets 32. møbeludstilling, fredag, den 19. September 1958", DMD Arkiv 14 (Christiansen).

35   Michael Ellison, *Designed for Life: Scandinavian Modern Furnishings 1930–1970* (Pennsylvania: Schiffer Publishing Ltd., 2002), 12.

36   "Mobilia Scandinavia: Fight Against the Plagiarisms," *Mobilia*, n.s., nos. 35/36 (June/July 1958), v.

37   Hart (Martin Hartung), "Pinlig Plagiat-Affære på Møbel-Udstillingen," *B.T.*, October 1, 1955; Hart (Martin Hartung), "Al Sagkundskab vil nu modes om Plagiat-Affæren, *B.T.*, October 3, 1955; V. A. Engel, "Usentimental Stol," *B.T.*, October 4, 1955.

38   Hart (Martin Hartung), "Soveværelse et Skab," *B.T.*, September 30, 1955.

39   Hart (Martin Hartung), "Pinlig Plagiat-Affære."

40   Hart (Martin Hartung), "Pinlig Plagiat-Affære."

41   "Increasing the Turnover of a Furniture Export" [interview with Fearnley France], *Mobilia*, n.s., no. 24 (May 1957), n.p.

42   Svend Erik Møller, "The Danish Furniture production has always been based on the skilled cabinet-maker," in *The Furniture Fair Denmark 1963* (pamphlet), 1963, n.p.

43   "Møbler som Mærkervarer," *Mobilia* 21, no. 7 (July 1955): n.p.

44   "Møbler som Mærkervarer," *Mobilia* 21, no. 7 (July 1955): n.p.

45   "Mobilia Scandinavia: Fight against the Plagiarisms," *Mobilia*, n.s., nos. 35/36 (June/July 1958), v.

46   Danish Judgement Register, U.1960.483Ø, 488. Quoted in Stina Teilmann-Lock, *The Object of Copyright: A Conceptual History of Originals and Copies in Literature, Art and Design* (New York: Routledge, 2016), 137.

47   Edgar Kaufmann Jr., "Hans Wegner: The Heresies of a Quiet Dane," *Industrial Design*, March 1959, 58.

48   "Betænkning om lovforslag om ophavsretten til litterære og kunstneriske værker m.m," *Folkettingstidende*, Tillæg B, 1960–61., Sp. 628f, quoted in Teilmann-Lock, *Object of Copyright*, 137.

49   Jens Schovsbo, Morten Rosenmeier, and Clement Salung Petersen, *Immaterialret: Ophavsret, Patentret, Brugsmoderet, Designret, Varemærkeret* [3rd edition] (Copenhagen: Jurist- og Økonomforbundets forlag, 2013), 74ff, quoted in Teilmann-Lock, *Object of Copyright*, 138.

50   Danish Judgement Register, U.1961.1027H, 1030, quoted in Teilmann-Lock, *Object of Copyright*, 139.

51   Danish Judgement Register, U.1961.1027H, 1032, quoted in Teilmann-Lock, *Object of Copyright*, 140.

52   "Once Upon a Time There Were Two Chairs Which Resembled Each Other," *Mobilia*, n.s., no. 29 (November/December 1957), 40.

53   Danish Judgement Register, U.1960.483Ø, 488. Quoted in Teilmann-Lock, *Object of Copyright*, 137.

54   "Designed and Made in the U.S.A.," 89.

55   "Changing Times," *Kiplinger's Personal Finance* (January 1969), 30.

56   "Danish Furniture," *Mobilia* 22, no. 7 (July 1956): 6.

57   Michael Sheridan, *The Furniture of Poul Kjærholm: Catalogue Raisonee* (New York: Gregory R. Miller, 2007), 44.

58   "Københavns Snedkerlaugs 34. Møbeludstilling's åbning, fredag, den 16. sept. 1960," DMD Arkiv 14 (Christiansen).

59   "Den Permanente SU44, Strüwing 50–135; Udstillingen Design i Textil 1962," Den Permanente Arkiv, Erhversarkivet, Aarhus.

60   See, for example, "Københavns Snedkerlaugs 33. Møbeludstilling's åbning fredag, den 18. sept. 1959."; "Københavns Snedkerlaugs 34. Møbeludstilling's åbning, fredag, den 16. sept. 1960"—both DMD Arkiv 14 (Christiansen).

61   Johannes Hansen, "Om møbeleksporten," *Snedkermestrenes Medlemsblad* 57, no. 1 (January 1957), 5,

62   See, for example, D., "Møbelmessen i Fredericia," *Møbler* 32, no. 6 (June 1955), 19–22.

63   "Modern Group for Custom Offices," *Baker Bugle* 15, no. 3 (January 1958): 1.

64   Edgar Kaufmann Jr., *Prize Designs for Modern Furniture* (New York: Museum of Modern Art, 1950), 71; Christian Holmsted Olesen, *Wegner: Just One Good Chair*, trans. Mark Mussari (Ostfildern: Hatje Cantz, 2014), 159, 161–64.

65   "En haandsnedker bruger da maskiner," *Politiken*, February 20, 1955.

66   Finn Juhl to Niels Vodder (letter, November 30, 1966), DMD Arkiv 120 (Juhl).

67   *Berlingske Aftenavis*, quoted in Jalk, *40 Years of Danish Furniture Design*, 4:313.

Afterword

1   Christian Holmsted Olesen, *Wegner: Just One Good Chair*, trans. Mark Mussari (Ostfildern: Hatje Cantz, 2014), 165.

2   Finn Juhl, "Sådan bor man: I "fremtidens bolig," *Møbler* 31, no. 11 (1954): 29.

3   Juhl, "Sådan bor man," 31.

4   Charles D. Gandy and Susan Zimmermann-Stidham, *Contemporary Classics: Furniture of the Masters* (New York: McGraw-Hill, 1982), 114.

5   Steen Eiler Rasmussen, "Furniture—Tools of Living," *Danish Foreign Office Journal: Special Issue for the United States* (1955), 24.

6   Rachel, "Kik i Krogene," *Ekstrabladet*, September 19, 1959.

7   Betty Pepis, "Danish Furniture Features Chairs," *New York Times*, November 19, 1952, 34.

8   Fr. Brahtz, "Småplunk om Oliebehandling," *Møbler* 32, no. 6 (1955), 29–31; David Greenberg to Asger Fischer (letter, October 19, 1953), DMD Arkiv 119 (Fischer).

9   Knud Poulsen, "The Tea-tray," *1965, Københavns Snedkerlaugs 39. udstilling*, DMD Arkiv 14 (Christiansen).

10 Advertisement, 1968, Annoncescrapbøger 1968–1979, Den Permanente Collection, Erhvervsarkivet, Aarhus, Denmark.

Further Reading (in English)

Ashby, Charlotte. *Modernism in Scandinavia: Art, Architecture, and Design*. London: Bloomsbury Academic, 2017.

Bundegaard, Christian. *Finn Juhl: Life, Work, World*. London: Phaidon, 2019.

Davies, Kevin, "Markets, Marketing and Design: The Danish Furniture Industry c. 1947–65," *Scandinavian Journal of Design History* 9 (1999): 56–73.

Dybdahl, Lars. *Furniture Boom: Mid-Century Danish Furniture, 1945–1975*. Translated by Dorte Herholdt Silver. Copenhagen: Strandberg Publishing, 2018.

Fallan, Kjetil, ed. *Scandinavian Design: Alternative Histories*. London: Berg, 2012.

Gelfer-Jørgensen, Mirjam. *Furniture with Meaning: Danish Furniture 1840–1920*. Translated by W. Glyn Jones. Copenhagen: Danish Architectural Press, 2009.

———. *Influences from Japan in Danish Art and Design 1870–2010*. Translated by Cornelius Holck Colding. Copenhagen: Danish Architectural Press, 2013.

Givens, Jean A. "Craft, Commerce and Den Permanente," *Design and Culture* 7, no. 3 (2015): 335–56.

Guldberg, Jørn. "'Scandinavian Design' as Discourse: The Exhibition *Design in Scandinavia*, 1954–57." *Design Issues* 27, no. 2 (Spring 2011): 41–58.

Halén, Widar, and Kerstin Wickman, ed. *Scandinavian Design beyond the Myth: Fifty Years of Scandinavian Design from the Nordic Countries*. Stockholm: Arvinius Forlag/Form Förlag, 2003.

Hansen, Per H. *Danish Modern Furniture, 1930–2016: The Rise, Decline and Reemergence of a Cultural Market Category*. Translated by Mark Mussari. Odense: University Press of Southern Denmark, 2018.

———. *Finn Juhl and His House*. Translated by Mark Mussari. Ostfildern: Hatje Cantz, 2014.

————. "Networks, Narratives, and New Markets: The Rise and Decline of Danish Modern Furniture Design, 1930–1970." *Business History Review* 80 (Autumn 2006): 449–83.

Ifversen, Karsten R. S., and Birgit Lyngbye Pedersen. *Finn Juhl at the UN—a Living Legacy*. Foreword by Michael Sheridan. Translated by Martha Gaber Abrahamsen. Copenhagen: Strandberg Publishing, 2013.

Jalk, Grete. *40 Years of Danish Furniture Design*. 4 vols. Translated by Alex Rose. Copenhagen: Teknologisk Instituts Forlag, 2017.

Karlsen, Arne. *Danish Furniture Design in the 20th Century*. 2 vols. Translated by Martha Gaber Abrahamsen. Copenhagen: Christian Ejlers' Forlag, 2007.

Leary, Erin. "'The Total Absence of Foreign Subjects': The Racial Politics of US Interwar Exhibitions of Scandinavian Design," *Design and Culture* 7, no. 3 (2015): 335–56.

Lowry, Vicky. *Jens Risom: A Seat at the Table*. Berlin: Phaidon, 2022.

Massey, Anne. *Chair*. London: Reaktion, 2011.

Müller, Michael. *Børge Mogensen: Simplicity and Function*. Translated by Mark Mussari. Berlin: Hatje Cantz, 2016.

Munch, Anders V., and Hans-Christian Jensen. "Selling Time: Multiple Temporalities in the Promotion of Danish Design Classics." *Journal of Design History* (2021). https://doi.org/10.1093/jdh/epab038

Mussari, Mark. *Danish Modern: Between Art and Design*. London: Bloomsbury Academic, 2016.

Olesen, Christian Holmsted. *Wegner: Just One Good Chair*. Translated by Mark Mussari. Ostfildern: Hatje Cantz, 2014.

Osvald, Lise. "The Story of Kaj Dessau's BO, 1928–1941: A Domicile for Scandinavian Design." *Scandinavian Journal of Design History* 3 (1993): 19–40.

Penick, Monica. *Tastemaker: Elizabeth Gordon, House Beautiful, and the Postwar American Home*. New Haven, CT: Yale University Press, 2017.

Rybczynski, Witold. *Now I Sit Me Down: From Klismos to Plastic Chair, a Natural History*. New York: Farrar, Straus and Giroux, 2016.

Selkurt, Claire. "Scandinavian Modern Design in Postwar America." *Form,*

Funktion, Finland 2 (1990): 35–43.

Sheridan, Michael. *The Furniture of Poul Kjaerholm: Catalogue Raisonne*. New York: Gregory R. Miller, 2007.

———. *Room 606: the SAS House and Work of Arne Jacobsen*. London: Phaidon, 2003.

Sommer, Anna-Louise. *Watercolors by Finn Juhl*. Translated by James Manley. Berlin: Hatje Cantz, 2016.

Taft, Maggie. "Morphologies and Genealogies: Shaker Furniture and Danish Design." *Design and Culture* 7, no. 3 (2015): 313–34.

Teilmann-Lock, Stina. "Danish Design: Legal Restrictions and Creative Responses." *Design and Culture* 6, no. 3 (2014): 291–302.

Thompson, Jane, and Alexandra Lange. *Design Research: The Store That Brought Modern Living to American Homes*. San Francisco: Chronicle Books, 2010.

Tigerman, Bobbye, and Monica Obniski, eds. *Scandinavian Design and the United States, 1890–1980*. New York: Prestel, 2020.

Wilson, Kristina. *Mid-Century Modernism and the American Body: Race, Gender, and the Politics of Power in Design*. Princeton, NJ: Princeton University Press, 2021.

Index

Page numbers in italics refer to illustrations.

73–74, 138, *pl. 1*, *pl. 3*, *pl. 4*; fabrication
methods, 53, 54, 55, 74; sales, 37, 120,
126
Vogue (magazine), 64, 65, *pl. 8*

Wanscher, Wilhelm, 29
Washington Post, 72
Wegner, Hans: collaboration with Fritz
Hansen, 26, 29, 30; collaboration with
Johannes Hansen, 25, 26, *27*, 35, 29, 56,
61, 122, 135–36, *137*, 144, *pl. 2*; copies,
111, 113, 114, 121, 122–24, 127–28, 129,
145; on design of Round Chair, 25–26,

27, 30, *31*, 121; designs (excl. Round
Chair), 25–26, 43, 55–56, 100, 106, 111,
124, 126, 135–36, *137*; education, 26–30;
in press, *90*, 91, 99, 100, 112, 114, 119,
128, *pl. 6*, *pl. 7*; reputation, 8, 51, 64;
use of materials, 66, 135–36, 144
Westinghouse, 115
world's fairs: Paris (1900), 28; New York
(1939), 44, 52, 79, 83–84, 142
Wright, Frank Lloyd, 48, 78, 92

Zacho (store), 7
Zenith Radio Corporation, 115